Sport BrandLeaders

AN INSIGHT INTO SOME OF BRITAIN'S STRONGEST SPORTS BRANDS

Argentina • Australia • Brazil • Canada • Czech Republic • Denmark • Egypt • Finland, France • Germany
Greece • Hong Kong • Hungary • India • Indonesia • Ireland • Italy • Japan • Kuwait • Lebanon • Malaysia
Morocco • Mexico • The Netherlands • Norway • Pakistan • Philippines • Poland • Portugal • Russia
Saudi Arabia • Singapore • South Africa • South Korea • Spain • Sweden • Taiwan • Thailand • Turkey
United Arab Emirates • United Kingdom • United States

MANAGING EDITOR
Angela Pumphrey

AUTHORS
Drew Barrand
Chris Britcher
James Curtis

PICTURE EDITOR
Emma Selwyn

DESIGNER
Adrian Morris

BRAND LIAISON DIRECTORS
Simon Muldowney
Claire Pollock

Other publications from Superbrands in the UK;
Superbrands 2004 ISBN: 0-9547510-0-0
Business Superbrands 2004 ISBN: 0-9541532-6-X
Cool BrandLeaders 2004 ISBN: 0-9547510-1-9

For Superbrands publications dedicated to: Argentina, Australia, Brazil, Canada, Czech Republic, Denmark, Egypt,
Finland, France, Germany, Greece, Hong Kong, Hungary, India, Indonesia, Ireland, Italy, Japan, Kuwait, Lebanon,
Malaysia, Morocco, Mexico, The Netherlands, Norway, Pakistan, Philippines, Poland, Portugal, Russia, Saudi Arabia,
Singapore, South Africa, South Korea, Spain, Sweden, Taiwan, Thailand, Turkey, United Arab Emirates,
United Kingdom, United States email brands@superbrands.org or call 020 7379 8884.

To order a copy of Sport BrandLeaders please call 01825 723398

© 2004 Superbrands Ltd

Published by Superbrands Ltd
19 Garrick Street
London
WC2E 9AX

www.superbrands.org/uk

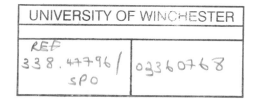

Printed in Italy ISBN: 0-9547510-4-3

JOHN NOBLE Director, British Brands Group

The British Brands Group is delighted to support Sport BrandLeaders. The brands here may be diverse but all have achieved a fame that reaches well beyond the particular sports they serve. To achieve such fame, they have had to perform outstandingly, be consistent, and strike a deep rapport. They have had to do this over years and years. The collection shows how brands touch us all. For their users, the relationship is deep and personal. For others, they are leaders in their field, examples of excellence, and a source of admiration. Some brands here have gone further still, to become icons of contemporary culture and the focus of patriotic fervour, part of the national identity. It is great to see such performance recognised and celebrated. The Brands Group works to encourage more of such brands to come to the fore, bringing us choice, diversity and spice to our lives.

PAUL GOSTICK International Chairman, The Chartered Institute of Marketing (CIM)

Brands have become central to our everyday lives and most of us cannot fail to be touched by them. The most powerful brands have become so well known that they are embedded in the hearts of millions and have developed their own personalities. That personality makes a brand more interesting and memorable and can become a vehicle to express a customer's identity, particularly in sport. Sport is able to transcend many boundaries and people look forward to major sporting events each year. Therefore it is not surprising that for the sports fan brands are especially powerful. The case studies in Sport BrandLeaders have been developed to give people greater insight into many of our nation's most powerful sporting entities. CIM is delighted to endorse this publication, which showcases sportswear manufacturers, sporting events and sporting venues. The brands in this book will bring back many sporting memories to the nation.

TESSA GOODING Communications Director, Institute of Practitioners in Advertising (IPA)

This latest book from the Superbrands stable is a testament to the importance of sport as a communications category in its own right and is a welcome addition to the series. The case histories outlined in this new book give us new insights into a number of iconic images, people and places that these days can't help but dominate our consciousness. Our sporting hero's, past and present have given us all moments to remember, but their influence over recent years, both in terms of ability and celebrity, is surely remarkable and arguably has given rise to what we know now as the sporting Superbrand. I am sure that this will be the first of many such books from this most excellent of organisations and the IPA is very happy to endorse it.

ROGER DRAPER Chief Executive, Sport England

Sport England is the organisation providing the strategic lead for the delivery of the Government's sporting agenda in this country, and is a distributor of lottery funds to sport. Our mission is: to work with others to create opportunities for people to get involved in sport, to stay in sport, and to excel and succeed in sport at every level. We are very conscious of the importance of branding in the world of sport and as we go through our own period of modernisation and reorganisation, are taking time to consider what it is we stand for, how we are uniquely different, and how we want to convey this and the value we add, to our customers. Therefore we are delighted to be associated with this collection of the best in sports branding – the brands that have managed to create those key points of differentiation and in doing so, created an enduring rapport with their customers. We hope other readers will find us much insight here as we have done.

This is the first edition of Sport BrandLeaders and is part of a pioneering and exciting programme that was founded with the aim of paying tribute to many of the UK's strongest sport brands.

A dedicated Sport BrandLeaders Council (listed below) has been formulated consisting of eminent individuals who are well qualified to judge which are the nation's strongest sport brands. Each brand featured in this book has qualified to be showcased based on the ranking of this Council.

Through identifying these brands, and providing their case histories, the organisation hopes that people will gain a greater appreciation of the discipline of branding and a greater admiration for the brands themselves.

Beyond this branding bible, the Sport BrandLeader programme encompasses a dedicated website and Tribute Event, as well as other events about sport branding and constant appearances by representatives of Superbrands on TV, radio and in newspapers commenting upon branding.

Sport BrandLeaders Council

TONY ALLEN
Managing Director
Fortune Street

HUGH BIRLEY
Chief Executive
Lexis Public Relations

MARZENA BOGDANOWICZ
Director of Marketing
British Olympic Association

PETER BROOKING
Marketing Manager
Ducati UK

SABIN BROOKS
Sports Marketing Controller
for Sky/Sky Sports
British Sky Broadcasting Group

ROGER DRAPER
Chief Executive
Sport England

KAREN EARL
Managing Director
Karen Earl Sponsorship

RICHARD GILLIS
Freelance Journalist

NICK KELLER
Managing Director
Benchmark Sport &
the Sport Industry Awards

GABBY LOGAN
Presenter of ITV 1's
Champions League Coverage

STEVE MADINCEA
Founder & Group Managing
Director
PRISM

ALISTAIR PHILLIPS
Group Editor
SGB Publications

ANDY RUBIN
Chief Executive
Pentland Brands

RICHARD SUTTON
Editor
Sports Industry Magazine

GRAHAM WALPOLE
Head of Consulting (Europe)
IMG

CONTENTS

ANGELA PUMPHREY
Managing Editor

Sport. It immediately means something to everyone – whether it's winning or losing; a school competition or a world title – the memories are just as vivid either way. It is incredible to think how sport can stir not only individuals but whole nations with a sense of pride and belonging or intense frustration and disappointment. The loyalty that accompanies this range of emotions is also staggering, and for the branding world most enviable.

It is therefore a forceful blend when the worlds of branding and sport collide, with the passion and commitment sparked by sport and the emotional and physical benefits of strong branding being brought together. Those who successfully mix the qualities of a product or service with a set of brand values that consumers respect, will create a Sport BrandLeader that people truly believe is best in its field.

This publication delves into some of the Sport BrandLeaders that have reached this admirable position and examines how they got there, what they stand for and where they are going next. Only brands that have been highly rated, by the independent and voluntary Sport BrandLeader Council were considered for inclusion in this publication. It should be noted that Council members do not vote for any brand that they have an association with. In addition, many teams and personalities can, arguably, be considered as Sport BrandLeaders, but we have focused on products and services in this publication. These inspiring icons will however be a key part of the wider research element of the Sport BrandLeaders programme.

The council, which consists of eminent figures from the world of sport and branding have also given an insight into How to Build a Sport BrandLeader in pages that follow.

But do remember, its all about the taking part!

HOW TO BUILD A SPORT BRANDLEADER
according to the Sport BrandLeaders Council

STEPHEN CHELIOTIS

Brand Liaison Director
Superbrands
Chair Sport BrandLeaders Council

TONY ALLEN

Managing Director
Fortune Street

In the beginning, demonstrate a sports focus and proven performance. It's about tangibles. Don't be distracted by image making. People will find you and make your image for you. Your brand will be featured in the 'pro' end of the market. From here it's much easier to roll downhill into the mass market.

Staying the pace is the hard bit. Flirting too much with fashion can lead to a loss of perceived integrity.

Besides that, 'under-professionalise' your branding. Be very cool with your first customers – treat them like the ambassadors they will be for your brand. Help them by telling your product story well. They found you and they deserve the chance to brag about you.

Most of all, remember the principle of the natural (and legal) high – you only get the benefit of endorphin release by progressively harder exertion. This rule applies to sports brands as much as it does to sportspeople.

HUGH BIRLEY

Chief Executive
Lexis Public Relations

Whether the target is fitness freaks or armchair fans, all aspirant Sport BrandLeaders try to sell the associated thrills of competitive sport, the winning or sense of belonging, with their products. But sport brands become Sport BrandLeaders only when they consistently deliver genuine innovation and functional benefit. Nike's best brand defence and support has been constant innovation, from the waffle air sole to 'sharkskin' swimming suits and rugby jerseys which deliver additional performance for the athletes that have tested, developed and endorsed them and which are bought by millions of us. Helly Hansen builds life-saving ocean racing suits; Patagonia's fishing jackets remain impervious after hours spent in torrential rain; adidas makes boots that bend it for Beckham. Sport BrandLeaders remain beacons of refreshing honesty; like few other consumer goods, they deliver a unique combination of rational and emotional benefit when it really matters. This will continue to set the sector apart and make it compelling for consumers and the non-sport brands and businesses desperate to join in.

MARZENA BOGDANOWICZ

Director of Marketing
British Olympic Association

What is a sports brand, how is it defined? Is it a brand that can extend itself into sport and then become a 'sports brand' or is it a brand that is the sport or product itself? Is the London Marathon, Wimbledon or the Olympic Games a sports brand? Is adidas, the Barclaycard Premiership or the Stella Artois Championships a sports brand?

Each is different; some are a sports product, some a sports event, others are an extension of a sponsor into the sport/event. To build a Sport BrandLeader there needs to be credibility and emotion within the sports brand, the brand must be identifiable within the immediate sporting environment and thereafter command its own position among the public or consumers. A true Sport BrandLeader has the respect of those who participate and those who watch, whether it is an event, a product or activity.

ROGER DRAPER

Chief Executive
Sport England

Know your audience, know what you stand for, have a unique proposition communicate it well. And as time moves on, evolve your brand to changing market conditions. When I think of the classic sport brands they seem to fit with the above. From individual icons to community clubs, from the things we like to wear to publications we like to read, from the events we like to attend to the competitions we like to follow, from the equipment we like to use – and so on. Some of the great sport brands such as Wimbledon and adidas seem to have been with us forever. Others such as David Beckham have arrived more recently. The phenomenon of the Beckham brand is hardly ever off the front pages, but I think we still claim him as a Sport BrandLeader. Just. The importance of uniqueness should not be underestimated, particularly to deliver that initial breakthrough. Think of TaylorMade golf clubs – a new dimension in style and individuality, JJB sports with a new retail model and the Observer Sport Monthly for a new standard and style for informed feature writing on a Sunday. But these weren't innovations for innovations sake. They saw a market and capitalised. And Sport BrandLeaders keep moving with the times. Nike – with a style of sports shoe for every activity. Speedo – with millisecond saving revolutions in swimwear. And so it goes on. Sport BrandLeaders don't rest on their laurels.

KAREN EARL

Managing Director
Karen Earl Sponsorship

To build a Sport BrandLeader marketers need to reach consumers through their passion – sport. Understanding that passion is key to success or failure. Savvy marketers know they need to seek permission to enter this prized, personal space. They need to show a deep-rooted understanding of the sport and the passion it generates amongst its fans. Get it wrong and a brand can be dead and buried in no time. Get it right and the sky's the limit.

Sports fans very quickly see through brands which use sport as a commercial vehicle – as a walking, talking billboard if you like. These brands will not be accepted as true leaders and won't gain iconic status.

Thus, a true Sport BrandLeader has effectively demonstrated its consummate support, not only at the pinnacle but right through to the grassroots of a sport. It provides tangible proof that the brand's presence is enhancing consumers' enjoyment.

RICHARD GILLIS

Freelance Journalist

I can recall very few people referring to Manchester United as a brand in the 1980s, when they had Garry Birtles wandering around upfront seeking a cow's arse with a banjo. But that doesn't mean they weren't one, Man U has always been a great brand — they just didn't make as much money from it then. They are the most loved, and hated, club in the world and they split opinion because they stand for something. There is an idea behind the badge. Every chairman in the Premiership would give his camel coat to be as despised as Manchester United.

We now routinely refer to the club as a model of sports marketing excellence, but this is a judgement taken against a period of almost unbroken on-the-field success.

This emphasises both the potential of sports brands, and their fragility. The message to those seeking to build one of their own is clear. Stand for something. And keep winning.

NICK KELLER

**Managing Director
Benchmark Sport & the
Sport Industry Awards**

Emotion creates brands. None more so than in the wonderful world of Sport. Ask a consumer how they feel about their morning cereal or their washing powder and they will say they 'like it'. But how far does their loyalty really go? A shift in quality or price is likely to see the product fall by the wayside. In sport though loyalty is irrational. Ask a sports fan about 'their team' or 'their star player' or 'their lucky shirt'. Their eyes light up, their hair stands on end and they will speak from

the heart with passion and emotion. When we talk about sports brands we talk with proximity and an understanding that feels like ownership. We support failing teams, poor performing stars, attend events that invariably do not deliver and wear kit that has been far superseded. A good sports brand recognises that you cannot take the consumers raw unbridled emotion for granted and continues to push the boundaries.

GABBY LOGAN

**Presenter of ITV 1's
Champions League Coverage**

If I was setting out to create the next big Sport BrandLeader my main focus would be on credibility. Sports fans are a particularly critical and knowledgeable group of consumers, whether it is the TV they watch, the trainers they buy or the teams they align themselves to. They can spot a fake at a hundred paces. History in your market place seems to buy you a great deal of flexibility and support, hence adidas' ability to bring back trainers that are close to 30 years old. They have retro status as well as being cutting edge in the technology of their most technical equipment

e.g. football boots. The same can be said of Nike, who have clothing lines which appear to be based on 1970s college strips. Of course, unlike the adidias Gazelle trainers, these items didn't exist in the 1970s but still they are able to pass them off because the consumer trusts them. I think being at the edge of technology is very important for the consumer. If they are paying over £100 for a pair of football boots they do not want to feel that there is another pair down the High Street which is more advanced. Style is increasingly important and if you are sponsoring and endorsing sportsmen you need to be sure the right people are wearing your clothes and apparel. Above all it helps if the people who wear your goods are winners as there can be no greater positive impact than that. Not so long ago sportswear used to be functional, now it has to function and look amazing. Knowledge is the key to all of these. Know who you are pitching to and how you are going to distinguish yourself from the next guy.

STEVE MADINCEA

**Founder & Group Managing
Director
PRISM**

Brands with rational consumer relationships choose sports to create a stronger, more lasting emotional relationship with those consumers. An overlooked element in building this powerful bond through sports is the element of competition.

Sports are competitive and being involved in sports sets out a brand as striving to be more successful than its competitors. The more a brand can show its competitive strengths via sports, the more the brand truly becomes a Sport BrandLeader. Think of Ferrari and Nike

but also Flora, Vodafone and HSBC, who continually use their sports associations to separate their brands from competitors while building stronger emotional relationships with their key customers.

Everyone loves a winner, and brands involved with sport are no exception. The true test is to use sports involvement to convert your brand attributes into a valued emotional relationship with your end user. Then success is yours!

ALISTAIR PHILLIPS

Group Editor
SGB Publications

Sports brands come and go very quickly. To establish a sports brand as a leader in its field, initially some sort of emotional connection has to be made with the consumer. Sport evokes emotions at all levels whether it's a game of darts with your mates down the pub or whether you are watching an Olympic athlete winning a gold medal. Once this emotional link is established, and enough consumers have a shared experience, that link has to be maintained over a long period of time – that's the difficult bit.

Getting the consumer to fall in love with the brand is no easy thing, but to turn that love affair into a long term relationship, a marriage if you will, means not only continuing to make that emotional connection but also serving up a product that is of high quality, and is constantly looking inwards as well as outwards, improving, innovating and modernising.

ANDY RUBIN

Chief Executive
Pentland Brands

Building a sports brand takes passion, patience and persistence. Passion because without this, nobody will believe in the cause, patience because it always takes longer than you think and persistence because there will be tough times along the way.

Sports brands need to be rooted in a limited number of core activities and devoted to their cause. To build credibility in the chosen activity requires knowledge and expertise. This comes from having athletes on the team and access to participants from grass roots through to elite levels.

At Pentland we own a number of brands operating in different sports: Mitre in football, rugby and netball, Speedo in acquatic sports, Berghaus® in outdoor activities and ellesse in tennis and ski. This allows us to focus those brands on their core activity without having to appeal across a very wide spectrum.

In order to appeal to consumers over a long period of time, brands must have clarity and consistency in their marketing message and there must be real integrity in products. Quality, durability and being 'fit for purpose' are paramount.

RICHARD SUTTON

Editor
Sports Industry Magazine

Assuming you've got a good (preferably a great) product, you also need a clear vision of who you are and where you are going. The top brands are distinctive and instantly recognisable, so be original and creative when building customer awareness. Remember that sport is all about passion, commitment, excitement and achievement, so wherever possible look to associate your brand with similarly positive and uplifting messages. The top brands work on our emotions and inspire loyalty – we want to be associated with them and are often willing to pay a premium in the process. Most importantly, you have to engender trust – which means living up to your promises and always being able to meet – and sometimes exceed – your customers' expectations. The very best brands seem to have an extra special, 'magic' ingredient. If I knew what that was, I wouldn't be wasting my time writing this stuff for a living.

GRAHAM WALPOLE

Head of Consulting (Europe)
IMG

Sports brands face two distinct challenges.

Firstly, a sports brand's values are defined almost exclusively through performance and behaviour. Traditional marketing communication can reinforce but rarely redefine those values. Every consumer owns a window into the world of sport where those values are acted out and commentated upon daily under the media microscope. There is no hiding place for a sports brand that ceases to perform, whether it be the sportsman who stops winning or whose 'other' life is exposed in the tabloids or the sporting equipment that no longer delivers victories.

Secondly, while exciting new commercial avenues have opened up to many sporting stakeholders, that same commercialism can also destroy brands built on the purity of human and sporting ideals. Wimbledon and Tiger Woods have embraced commercialism but on terms that have remained consistent with their respective values. Others have not.

Today's Sport BrandLeaders have excelled in addressing these dual challenges.

When, in 1948, Rudi and Adi fell out and went their separate ways, adidas was born.

adidas would remain in the control of the Dassler family until 1989. Six years later it became a publicly traded company on the stock exchange.

In 1997 it sent a very clear message to the industry of its intention to enter new areas when it acquired the Salomon Group. Changing its company name to adidas-Salomon AG, it saw the core adidas sectors combined with the Salomon range of skis, inline skates, adventure shoes and clothing. It also provided adidas with a major slice of the golfing market, with TaylorMade, in addition to cycling brand Mavic and snowboard label Bonfire.

Achievements

By the time of his death in 1978, Adi Dassler had amassed more than 700 patents and other industrial property rights, as he sought to put the brand at the cutting edge; among his many firsts being the design of the first football boot with screw-in studs.

It is that urge to be the best which has gone a considerable way to ensuring the adidas brand remains at the forefront of its sector; an urge embedded within the very heart of its philosophy.

Background

In one of the most fiercely competitive sectors of the sport industry, the desire to secure increased market share has propelled adidas into becoming a clothing and equipment colossus – and one of the biggest and boldest brands on the planet.

With a firm commitment to sport sponsorship and endorsements, adidas has developed a brand loyalty built on a consistent image and investment delivered through a variety of different media and what it perceives as a clear commitment to the sports in which it is involved.

It is all a far cry from the village of Herzogenaurach in Bavaria where, in the 1920s, Adi Dassler, son of a local cobbler, created his first sports shoe. Along with his brother Rudi, Dassler founded the company Gebr. der Dassler Schuhfabriken.

A keen athlete himself, Adi Dassler set out with the goal of designing a shoe which would best serve the requirements of the sportsman or woman as they strived for success; a core brand value which continues to this day.

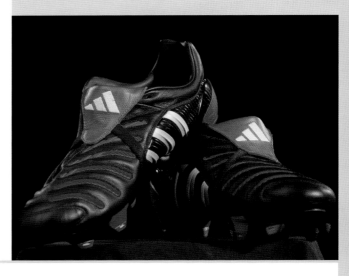

Striving to be the world's ultimate sports brand – leading the industry in products, in innovations, in sports and in the care of its athletes

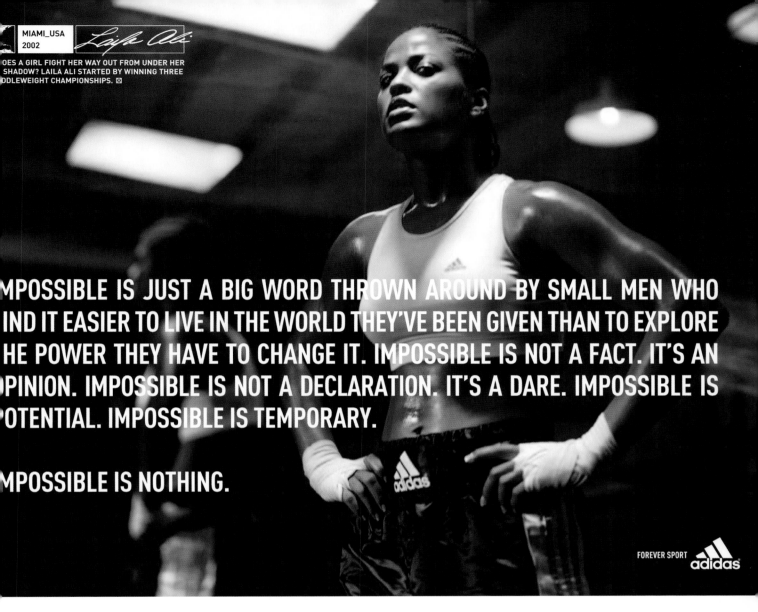

After a spate of year on year sales declines during the 1980s, adidas showed it was as adept at formulating sophisticated marketing campaigns as it was designing footwear.

Boosting its image, efficiency, turnover and market share saw it not only become the market leader in sportswear clothing, but by the late 1990s, one of the biggest spending consumer brands. Meanwhile, as a result of a carefully targeted campaign aimed at recapturing the imagination of a young and fashion conscious demographic it emerged in the 21st century as one of the fastest emerging 'youth' brands.

Product/Promotion

Today adidas targets three groups of sport-orientated consumers. Its Sport Performance division is aimed at athletes at all performance levels. Sport Heritage targets trendsetters seeking sport-inspired streetwear, while Sport Style focuses on young cosmopolitan consumers looking for exclusive, fashion-oriented sportswear products. The unifying way to access that consumer base is through sport.

The likes of football's David Beckham and Zinedine Zidane; golf's Sergio Garcia; swimming's Ian Thorpe; and sprinter Maurice Greene all help drive the brand's association with success at the highest level, alongside a massive programme of football team deals both at a domestic and international level.

Its 'Impossible is Nothing' recent brand push in 2004, which united sporting heroes from past and present, and across all continents, was hailed a huge success and represented its biggest brand advertising campaign in six years.

The brand is also a long-term sponsor of the FIFA World Cup, UEFA European Championships, and was an official supporter to the Athens 2004 Olympic Games, in addition to outfitting 22

www.adidas.com

National Olympic Committees.

From top-tier sponsorship to grassroots initiatives, media buys across all conceivable platforms ensure the way the adidas brand is marketed is almost as crucial to its success as the goods it produces.

animal®

Background

From humble beginnings as an accessory based product line for action sports enthusiasts, Animal has grown into an internationally recognised lifestyle brand.

The brand was originally conceived in 1987 by two surfers who were fed up with continuously losing their watches in the water due to the straps breaking under extreme conditions. Having developed a form of webbing and Velcro strap to counter this problem, the duo soon found that the product was in high demand. Originally targeting their fellow surfers, the nature of the strap made it suitable for crossing over into other action sports such as wind surfing, snowboarding and mountain biking and consequently the Animal brand was born. Over the years the product line has evolved from simple strapping to a range of clothing, eyewear, footwear, luggage and accessories.

Today Animal employs 150 people through an international headquarters and distribution centre as well as a growing retail division.

The evolution of the firm's logo perhaps best reflects the new positioning that this move from accessory led production, to being a fully fledged lifestyle brand has brought. In the 1980s, the logo had an aggressive feel with a 'home grown' look to it. However, as the brand's attitude has changed with the times, this hard feel has mellowed with more of a focus on enjoyment and fun not only of the sports themselves but also the lifestyle that is connected with them. The Animal brand name now appears in many different forms across the product range with no 'strict corporate rules' that limit the brand's creative appearance.

Achievements

Animal may have developed into a lifestyle brand that appeals to a consumer base beyond its traditional roots, but it remains a design-led company that is driven by its commitment to the action sports scene. Through close ties with UK surf, snow and bike enthusiasts and a number of retail partners, product design and development are central to the brand's evolution. One of the unique attributes that differentiates Animal from its competitors is its in-house design department with the entire creative output of the company being produced under one roof. Each designer is actively involved in the sports scene and works in tandem with the riders associated with the

Designed by Animals, tested on humans

brand to continuously refine and develop the best performing products. As a result, a number of the riders who act as ambassadors for the Animal brand, have been propelled to champion status.

Product/Promotion

As could be expected for a brand so closely aligned with the action sports scene, the bulk of Animal's marketing activity is centralised around its sponsorship of various team riders and sports events. Among the high profile riders aligned to Animal is the twice English national surfing champion Alan Stokes; renowned snowboarder and British Half Pipe champion Dom Harrington; and Kirsty Jones, British champion kitesurfer. All of the Animal riders are used extensively in the brand's marketing material including advertising in both the sports and lifestyle media, personal websites, in-store POS and packaging. In addition to the individual rider sponsorships, Animal also throws its brand weight behind a number of events in the free sports calendar, the most prestigious of which include the Animal Poole Windfest, a kitesurfing and windsurfing event now in its fourth year, and the Animal Beach Ball Tour – three two day televised surfing events taking place across Cornwall. Animal also promotes the grass roots side of free sports through its own Surf Academy.

The brand's now famous strapline – 'Designed by Animals, tested on humans' – underpins the values that Animal markets itself on, incorporating the passion for the free sports that drive the product line while acknowledging the lifestyle that has been born out of them.

www.animal.co.uk

athletics
WEEKLY

PHOTOGRAPHY: MARK SHEARMAN

Reviews the sport – Reveals the athlete

Background

For close to 60 years, Athletics Weekly has delivered the best in news, features, reviews, previews and comment for the followers of the UK's favourite Olympic sport. Known as the bible of the sport, athletes of every age affectionately call the title AW and the list of subscribers is a who's who of athletics in the UK.

Today, the magazine stands as the world's only remaining weekly track and field publication providing its loyal and evolving readership with 52 pages each week – expanding to 68 pages during the busy summer months.

An integral part of each issue is its comprehensive results service with a network of correspondents gathering reports and results from events as diverse as the junior schools cross-county championships to the Olympic Games, making the magazine a vital accessory for fans of sport at all levels.

The brand first left the starting blocks back in 1945 as an A5-sized title entitled simply 'Athletics'. To avoid post-war rationing restrictions founder Jimmy Green put 'volume two, number one' on the cover – a new magazine launch would have been prohibited.

In 1987, Green retired and sold the title to EMAP; a move which would see it switch to the more conventional A4 size.

Descartes Publishing, backed by owner Matthew Fraser Moat an athletic enthusiast and Great Britain athletics selector, took on the title under license in 1999, purchasing it outright in early 2004.

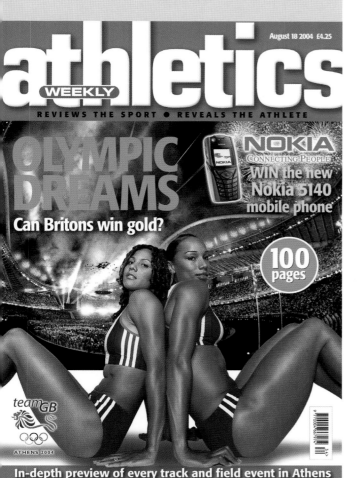

August 18 2004 £4.25

athletics
WEEKLY
REVIEWS THE SPORT ● REVEALS THE ATHLETE

OLYMPIC DREAMS
Can Britons win gold?

NOKIA
CONNECTING PEOPLE
WIN the new
Nokia 5140
mobile phone

100 pages

teamGB
ATHENS 2004

In-depth preview of every track and field event in Athens

Achievements

Athletics Weekly is the only weekly athletics magazine in the world. Its strength lies in the fact that no other country has the participation levels and competition structure to support a magazine that covers the whole sport from the grass roots to the elite.

Although many websites exist offering results services, coaching, news and features, very few can rival the centralised mine of information that Athletics Weekly provides. Its vast network of results contributors has often been imitated but its successful mix never matched.

The brand's core strength is that no one else has the rich heritage in the sport or experience in doing the job; a fact underlined by some of its contributors having worked on the title since the 1960s. Without exception, all staff on Athletics Weekly have ties with the sport either as competitors or life long enthusiasts.

Athletics Weekly revels in the loyalty of its readers. A recent reader survey showed that 86% of readers buy every issue and that 49% of readers have been buying the magazine for ten years or more. In this age of celebrity obsession and reality TV, the editorial team have refused to 'dumb down' the publication and 2004 saw AW deliver what many readers considered to be the 'best issue ever' – a bumper 84 page anniversary edition celebrating the 50th anniversary of the first four minute mile.

Subscription rates over the past three years have risen 60% on the back of a number of initiatives, with many of its loyal readership frequently showing their support and faith in the brand by opting for two year deals or more.

www.athletics-weekly.com

A new drive to target junior athletes with a discounted subscription rate also proved a big success, and introduced a new young demographic to its audience – one that will certainly appeal even more to its range of advertisers.

Product/Promotion

At the very centre of the brand's success has been its ability to cater for both those at the elite end of the sport and those at its grassroots. As a result, the brand's plentiful promotions and marketing are a carefully planned mix designed to target specific sectors of its audience.

Examples of this approach are demonstrated by sponsoring all grassroots national leagues, with all competitors and athletes receiving cut-price subscription offers. It also ensures it has a heavy presence at the major events with various distribution initiatives. In fact, it made such an impact during the World Indoor Athletics Championships in 2003 in Birmingham, despite having no official partnership with the event, that one national newspaper commented on the prolific showing it achieved.

A further key ingredient in its newsstand push is strategic television advertising. It takes place during the summer on British Eurosport around its coverage of athletics and has

proved crucial to driving sales and subscriptions around the large, high profile events.

Partnerships have been developed with UK Athletics, FastTrack, the sport's commercial agents London Marathon and the Great North Run, and excellent support from WH Smith in newsstand promotions, have allowed AW to cement its position as the sport's magazine of record.

The marvellous success of Kelly Holmes in the Athens Olympics and the London 2012 Olympic bid has dramatically increased the profile of the sport, inspiring a whole new generation of teenagers to start running, and thus become AW readers.

berghaus®
TRUST IS EARNED

Background

The Berghaus brand is inextricably linked with walking and climbing, courtesy of its range of clothing, rucksacks and footwear for the great outdoors.

Formed in 1966, the brand was born into a world when a day out on the hills or crags could often be spent without seeing a soul. It developed as outdoor pursuits became a popular pass-time, gaining its status and market position without compromising on the core functional values that underpinned its creation.

Then there were few rival brands delivering such specialist equipment, and it was this gap in the market which two keen climbers and mountaineers exploited when they opened the first specialist outdoor retail store in Newcastle-upon-Tyne.

The LD Mountain Centre quickly made its mark and joint founders Peter Lockey and Gordon Davison began to build its reputation.

A core part of the blossoming business was the importation of a range of products from mainland Europe for UK distribution. Playing on the demand then for quality German or Austrian products, the wholesale arm of the business took its name from a rough German translation of 'mountain centre' – and the Berghaus brand was born.

It did not take long before the founding duo began to design, test and make their own gear for sale in the shop, inspired by their own needs and requirements as end users.

Stamped with the Berghaus brand name, it sparked the reputation for being innovative, functional and of high quality.

Over the years the brand grew dramatically, and in 1993 its success attracted the Pentland Group which took Berghaus under its wing, playing a key part in its desire to develop a portfolio of world class, category-leading brands in sports, outdoors and fashion.

Achievements

For a company built on innovation it has delivered over the decades a number of sector influencing products. In 1972, it developed the first internal-framed rucksack, the Cyclops. Five years later it launched the first commercially available Gore-Tex jacket into Europe and cemented its position in the marketplace.

More recent additions include the phenomenally successful Extrem Light range and 2004's technical but stylish Adventure Travel collection.

A key achievement in further boosting its public image has been recruiting a number of the world's leading outdoor activists,

Providing ideal products that enhance the outdoor experience is at the heart of the brand. Trust is earned by the delivery of this objective

to flex, twist and pivot at all times and which therefore works with the body, rather than against it.

As it did with Cyclops over 30 years ago, and has done many times since, Berghaus is again poised to establish a benchmark product in a key category in its industry. In doing so, the company is set to rise further up the branding league table.

who have played important roles in testing gear and providing valuable feedback and knowledge to the product designers.

Climbers such as Sir Chris Bonington, Alan Hinkes, Alexander and Thomas Huber and Leo Houlding are all part of the Berghaus team, further reinforcing the brand message that its products are used by the very best and need to be the very best.

Product/Promotion

During 2001 Berghaus undertook a brand review that resulted in a new creative direction. Identifying that the trust it had developed over the years with its customers was at the very heart of the brand, a new marketing campaign was built around the statement 'Trust Is Earned'.

Backed up by an extensive advertising campaign which heavily showcased its sponsored climbers, this mantra drives through the very heart of what the brand offers and has been adopted throughout the business.

It has continued to build on the message as it continues to expand its range and keep ahead of its competitors.

In 2002, Berghaus broke new ground again when it launched Extrem Light to the trade; an integrated range of lightweight gear for multi-purpose outdoor use which remains at the forefront of the lightweight product revolution.

Extrem Light was supported with a suitably integrated marketing campaign, involving advertising, PR, a dedicated website, in-store support and a point-of-sale programme for retailers buying into the range.

When it arrived in store in February 2003, products sold out across Europe.

In an ever faster moving market, Berghaus continues to innovate right at the leading edge.

For 2005, it has developed BioFlex, a backpacking rucksack system that allows the wearer

www.berghaus.com

BLOC ®

Background

Bloc was founded in 1988 by Colin Pickering. He used his bedroom as a sales office and his garage as a warehouse.

Having previously worked for a large sunglasses distributor, Pickering had valuable experience of the sunglasses sector and identified a gap in the market for a high quality but affordable sports brand.

At a time when winter holidays were becoming popular and affordable to all, he saw the opportunity for dedicated winter frames, when most brands were focused on the summer market.

Pickering named the new brand Bloc. The name came from the question: 'What do sunglasses do?'

Sourcing products from manufacturers in Europe and the Far East, and taking time to research new technology and advancements in production materials, Pickering produced the initial range and designed the original Bloc logo and the first promotional materials himself.

The product was first presented to the outdoor trade at a show in Harrogate, North Yorkshire, from a tiny booth at the back of the hall.

BLOC represents high performance, cutting edge eyewear on a global scale

That day, Pickering only sold 100 glasses cords, worth just £20. However, this spurred him on to call every outdoor and sports retailer in the UK and within the first month 40 retailers were supporting the new brand.

Achievements

From the outset, Bloc revolutionised the ski and outdoor eyewear market. When many competing brands used the winter market as a dumping ground for unsold summer stock, Bloc was introduced as a winter sport-specific brand. This established a new category of sports sunglasses and its success is reflected in the rapid growth of the brand.

From humble beginnings, Bloc has built a diverse and far-reaching market, covering a whole spectrum of retail outlets all over the world, ranging from active sport and lifestyle through to department store chains.

Global distribution has grown across Europe, South America and Australia, with office and distribution centres opening in Melbourne, Australia and Wellington, New Zealand.

Bloc doesn't just have extensive reach, it is also one of the strongest performers in the sunglasses market at retail. In the majority of the stores it is sold in, Bloc sells more units and turns over more than any other collection, no matter the price, or brand.

Product/Promotion

From the outset, Bloc has offered affordable and desirable sports eyewear offering maximum protection from harmful UV rays.

Bloc is constantly refining and innovating designs, incorporating the latest fashions to give ultimate stylish performance, fit and protection in any conditions. Unlike many other sunglass brands, Bloc does not limit customer choice to one popular good fitting style, but offers fitted products for men, women and children

of all ages. Frames are designed for all different face shapes, while styles and fittings are varied to suit tastes in different countries.

Bloc frames are constructed of Nylon66™/TR90, a virtually indestructible and flexible material of extreme durability, while metal frames are Nickel free and hypo-allergenic. Both offer a comfortable close fit, with excellent peripheral vision.

All Bloc sunglasses use Karbon8™ shatterproof lenses, offering distortion-free vision and protection from harmful rays, as well as a high degree of blue light and infrared protection.

Since 2001, Bloc has expanded its range with the introduction of high-protection sun-cream highly suitable for snow and marine sports, performance goggles and gloves.

Bloc has also launched two new sub-brands – 'Nation' a fashion label for young style-hungry individuals and 'Zerodoublex' a range of eyewear for lifestyle and extreme sports utilising the very latest technologies.

Bloc invests in a full range of communication channels to support its market position and

growing product range. Over the years, the brand's effective use of marketing has helped achieve its now global reach.

Advertising has played a crucial role in the Bloc marketing mix, helping to communicate its sporting strength, and versatility. Bloc chooses its media carefully, for example using The Extreme Sports Channel on cable and satellite television, and print ads in magazines such as Adrenalin, Sports Illustrated and Daily Mail Ski and Snowboard.

Product placement on well-known television programmes has been used since 2000, with competitors wearing Bloc products on programmes such as Superstars and The World's Strongest Man as well as in the latest James Bond movie.

The brand also sponsors appropriate events, athletes and teams such as the UK Triathlon series, the elite skydiving squad - The Red Devils and Sam Connor, one of the world's leading motorcycle trials riders.

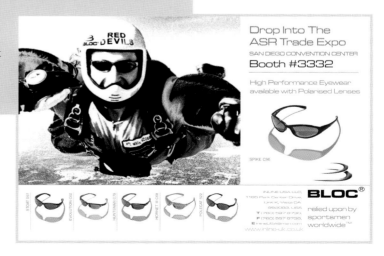

Background

The UK's maritime heritage stretches back centuries and has, over the years, produced some of the world's most prominent sailors and industry innovators.

For nearly the last 50 years, Crewsaver has played an increasingly important role in the billion-pound leisure maritime industry, developing and refining its range of safety equipment.

Today it is one of the market-leaders in a sector which exports 43% of its total annual sales of £1.83 billion, and sees its range of products used in more than 40 countries. No mean feat for a company designing and developing equipment it hopes its customers never need to use.

Looking back at the dawn of its creation in the 1960s, Crewsaver initially specialised in dinghy gear such as blocks, cleats, Bri-Nylon

clothing, lifejackets and buoyancy aids. Back in those days, safety equipment was strictly 'Board of Trade Approved', with designs harking back to the post-war utilitarian era. By 1967 the company was focusing on a range of safety gear, developing its own styles tailored to specific sectors of the sailing community.

Privately owned until 1983, its success and high profile saw it an oft-traded commodity which over the years saw it become part of a bedding manufacturer, a heating-to-locks conglomerate and then subject to a management buy-out.

But by 1997 company chiefs recognised the need for an injection of capital to help it

ensure its rate of growth was to be maintained.

To that end, the company was sold to Cosalt plc, a leading supplier to the commercial marine market; an obvious and natural match and one which continues to help fuel the brand's growth.

Achievements

After 20 years of establishing itself at the forefront of the safety sector, the mid 1980s proved a pivotal moment for Crewsaver.

Lifejacket technology was changing; the traditional, oral-inflation combined with solid-foam buoyancy designs, were bulky to wear and not meeting market demands for easy-to-

> A dedication to total quality, a continuous commitment to research and development, and a passion for getting things right

use equipment that functioned in the roughest conditions.

Crewsaver became pioneers in the design of new gas operated air-only lifejackets, which delivered many more feature-benefits as well as increasing overall safety for the user. It became the first manufacturer to launch a combined body harness and air-only lifejacket, closely followed in 1986 with the launch of its 'Crewfit' lifejacket range, which effectively established a worldwide benchmark for the design and function of lifejackets for the leisure user.

As a result, the brand became market dominant in the UK and, as featured in one particular ad campaign, 'Often copied but never equalled'.

Such was the company's expertise that during this period, personnel from Crewsaver were nominated to represent the UK on a European committee formulating new harmonised regulations for the design and manufacture of lifejackets. A position it still holds.

Product/Promotion

The Crewsaver portfolio currently boasts more than 170 types of product, ranging from core lifejacket models, to technical clothing; wetsuits; luggage; footwear and harnesses.

Used across a diverse range of environments, Crewsaver products can be found in places such as ocean cruising; oil exploration; dinghy racing; white water rafting; and search, rescue and security operations.

The brand has not rested on its laurels. When Crewsaver wanted to move into general water sports sectors; the fashion feel of the surf market; and somewhat 'off-the-wall' attitudes in the paddling community, it recognised it needed a different approach. As a result, brand extensions were devised which saw the launch of 'CSR Sport' and 'Yak' to service these specifics.

Most recently, the entire Crewsaver visual identity has been refreshed under the strapline 'Embracing the spirit of life'. The treatment will be rolled out over all aspects of the company's activities.

Although maintaining brand presence is crucial, Crewsaver also believes that it is important for the brand leader to provide general information and advice on the functioning and appropriate use of marine safety equipment. Thus, it goes to great lengths in promotional material to explain the differences between designs and how they should be used. For example, Crewsaver even provides an interactive multimedia CD, free, with all its Crewfit lifejackets.

www.crewsaver.co.uk

Crewsaver is also a significant sponsor of the various water sports its customers participate in, particularly helping youngsters to compete in events and develop their skills.

Background

With durability central to the Eastpak brand, it is unsurprising to learn that the company began life in 1960 as a manufacturer of military products such as duffel bags, ammunition pouches and knapsacks for the US Armed Forces. From these utilitarian beginnings under the moniker 'Eastern Canvas Products', the company transferred its attention to the consumer market in 1976 when it first produced a retail daypack line. At the end of the 1970s daypacks were still considered primarily a camping item. However, Mark Goldman, son of Eastpak founder Monte Goldman, pushed forward his vision of daypacks as a fashion and lifestyle accessory, introducing the Eastpak brand name at the turn of the decade. What initially accounted for less than 5% of the company's turnover, grew into a worldwide business over the following years with Eastpak becoming one of the first brands to cater for the emerging market of daypacks for young people. Over time, the product range has broadened to meet growing consumer interest with the introduction of flamboyant colours and prints making the Eastpak brand synonymous with style as well as functionality.

Achievements

The transition from accessory to lifestyle fashion product is where Eastpak has had the biggest impact. Having identified the opportunity within the youth market for the sale of daypacks, the introduction of new colours and prints to the product line has become the differentiator that places Eastpak apart from its market rivals. The approach to incorporate more colours and styles began in 1983 when Eastpak worked with fabric designer Roseanne Slavin to incorporate bright, bold, day-glo patterns into its daypacks, effectively promoting them as fashion accessories. Moving away from its traditional colours of olive, orange and camouflage, Eastpak revolutionised the market by successfully introducing shades such as lavender and plum.

Product/Promotion

The mix of progressive design combined with durable functionality is at the core of Eastpak's mission statement as it looks to meet the evolving needs and demands of today's active consumer. Eastpak has developed many technical features and fabrics with its products including the ability to hold snow and skateboards as well as pockets for technical gadgetry such as music players, laptops and cameras. The product range offers a variety of individual collections and innovative details, each focusing on specific lifestyle elements such as freesports, music or travel.

In the early 1980s, Eastpak decided to focus on the growing youth market for daypacks. It developed an intensive consumer advertising campaign, depicting

Built to resist

talent and growth in this area, including the annual Eastpak Transition Tour, a nationwide project that showcases the skills of its sponsored skateboard and BMX Team riders to aspiring followers of the sports.

Eastpak continues to work with innovative designers, artists and world-class athletes in the development of their products. Collaborations include Henk Schiffmaker (tattooist to the likes of Nirvana and the Red Hot Chilli Peppers), the 'Godfather of Graffiti' SEEN, urban artist Seak, D*Face and Kabe, Walter Van Beirendonck (the most anarchic of the infamous Antwerp Six) and Zombie Flesh Eaters – led by the twisted genius of Jamie Hewlett.

www.eastpak.com

its products as lifestyle essentials. Prior to this, many companies selling daypacks focused their marketing efforts on niche enthusiast channels. Much of Eastpak's marketing moved forward from this point and tackled a more mainstream audience. Continuing this lifestyle theme, it positioned its products as fun and exciting, not simply as functional necessities. These brand values have helped Eastpak to build up a strong association with freesports. Since 1986 Eastpak has embarked on a number of projects to encourage

ENGLAND RUGBY

Background

The game of rugby union was born in England in the early 19th century, with sixteen year-old Rugby schoolboy William Webb Ellis credited with catching the ball and running with it for the first time. With no formal rules, no referees and many versions of rugby being played in schools and clubs, injury was a growing problem. In 1870 a Richmond player died at a practice match and it became all too clear that somebody needed to take the game in hand.

And so in January 1871 delegates from 22 clubs met at London's Pall Mall restaurant and formed the Rugby Football Union (RFU). The Laws of the game, subsequently adopted, were much the same as those played at Rugby School. Indeed, the England team also adopted the white kit worn at the school. Although nobody is sure why the rose was added it seems likely that both the English royal rose and the red rose symbol on Rugby School's coat of arms were influential. The first mention of the distinctive rose emblem came in RFU Committee minutes in 1872.

Few of the pre-war players returned to international rugby after World War I and with a new kit issued, Alfred Wright designed a new rose, variations of which were used right up

until 1999. Recognising the need for a unique rose brand the RFU had a new graphic rose created in 1999. Made up of four colours, two reds and two greens this used with the organisation's title is a registered trade mark.

From the first ever international of England vs Scotland in March 1871, the game spread across the world remaining an entirely amateur sport until the tremendous success of the third Rugby World Cup made professionalism inevitable.

Achievements

England Rugby leapt from the back to the front pages of the newspapers in 2003 when,

after a nail biting final in Sydney, England won the Rugby World Cup.

The first northern hemisphere team to bring back the William Webb Ellis Trophy was greeted in the early autumn morning at Heathrow Airport by thousands of cheering fans. The elation was staggering, England had at last taken a top world sports title and the nation wanted to celebrate.

Product/Promotion

And celebrate it did, instantly capturing the attention of the world's press. As the squad and management held the trophy aloft on an open-top bus, more than a million supporters thronged the streets of London. They stood seven or eight deep on pavements, climbed lampposts, hung from windows and leapt into Trafalgar Square's fountains as the cavalcade arrived. Millions watched on TV as a suited and booted England squad were then entertained by the Queen at Buckingham Palace and the Prime Minister at 10 Downing Street.

The tremendous effect of winning the rugby world's top accolade brought gains throughout rugby. Rugby union soared into second place in sporting popularity according to MORI Sportstracker immediately after the World Cup win, compared to eighth

Rejuvenating pride not only in English Rugby but in English sport

position a year earlier. This meant that 15.66 million adults were interested in the game, a 50% increase.

The Sweet Chariot Tour took the William Webb Ellis Trophy to a million people over four months in a tour which included more than 300 events at rugby clubs, leisure and shopping centres throughout the land.

Sales soared at the Rugby Football Union's Rugby Stores and online, with shirts flying off the shelves and the month following the World Cup win brought in three quarters of a million pounds more than any previous month.

The England Sevens team is ranked second in the world, having won the Hong Kong 7s three times in a row and the IRB Emirates London 7s in two successive years. The U21s secured an impressive nine wins in ten games in their last season and the England U19s finished in their best ever position of fourth in the IRB World Championship.

England are World Cup Champions and the Webb Ellis Trophy has pride of place in Twickenham's Rugby Museum. Furthermore, Twickenham tickets are among the most sought after of all sporting and leisure events in the UK today.

www.rfu.com

Background

From the Olympics to the Tour de France, from international motorsports to world-class football, Eurosport delivers live, major international sporting events, backed by a unique depth of sports expertise, to a young, vibrant audience across Europe.

In just fifteen years, Eurosport has established itself as Europe's first and leading sport TV channel, providing pan-European exposure of more than 100 different sports to nearly 100 million homes.

Eurosport prides itself on its core broadcasting values: offering the biggest international events in their entirety, tailored to suit audiences across the continent and delivered in a variety of languages. At the same time, Eurosport has continued to stay true to its aim of being a young, dynamic, creative channel –

taking commercial initiatives and rolling out innovative promotional campaigns.

Created in 1989 by the European Broadcasting Union, and then backed in 1991 by France's leading commercial TV channel TF1, two years later it merged with the ESPN and Canal Plus channel, the European Sport Network, and in doing so became the only truly pan-European sports channel.

By 2001, TF1 and Canal Plus bought out ESPN's share of the company and, twelve months later, the French channel became the sole shareholder in the brand by acquiring the shares of Canal Plus.

Now wholly owned by TF1, and with the full support of its parent company, the channel is in a prime position to ensure it continues to be in a position to acquire the sporting rights which have made it such a success. Today Eurosport features in almost every cable and satellite operator's package of channels, delivering a menu of top sporting action from across the globe.

Achievements

In an increasingly competitive marketplace, where sport continues to act as a major driver in the subscription sales push of all the major cable and digital

platforms, Eurosport continues to hold a unique place in the sector with its cross-border appeal.

Today Eurosport is available in 98 million households – up from 33 million in 1991 – in 54 countries across Europe, broadcasting its programmes simultaneously in nineteen languages.

By acquiring key rights to key events, it now reaches 240 million viewers a year, with 95% receiving the channel in their local language. As a result, the brand proudly lays claim to being the most widely viewed channel in Europe.

With the flagship channel fully established, 2002 saw it launch a secondary sports information channel; Eurosportnews. This innovative sport news format, which marries television and internet sources, surpassed all expectations and is already available in 70 countries across Europe, Africa and Asia in five different languages, reaching fourteen million households, a figure which is rising all the time.

Backed up by its multinational, multilingual online operation – www.eurosport.com – it is little wonder the Eurosport brand has become synonymous with delivering the complete sports package, encouraging sports fans to get involved and 'feel the sport'.

But that's not all. The creation of specific 'local' channels such as British Eurosport has allowed the channel the flexibility to innovate and cater to the tastes and viewing habits of a particular nationality.

Eurosport's aim: to afford the widest access to the widest variety of sports to the widest possible audience

Studio-fronted programmes around sports with a 'British appeal' such as World Superbikes and certain carefully selected football matches, enable the station to provide tailored content and a British twist to broadcast material to supplement international programming.

Product/Promotion

Sport embodies positive values – passion, entertainment, excitement and commitment, which make it a powerful engagement. Eurosport continues to offer advertisers what it believes to be the best on-air pan-European solution to associating their brand with major sports events and the values associated with them.

With the highest audiences in pan-European TV, desirable audience profiles, a sports news TV service, online and mobile coverage, plus the world's biggest sporting events, a convincing argument is put before the media buyers of the many advertisers drawn to it.

As well as creative cross-platform advertising solutions, the channel promotes itself via strong creative media relations campaigns in addition to print trade and national advertising and on-site consumer facing activity.

In 2004, the EMS (European Media and Marketing Survey) confirmed and reinforced Eurosport's leading position in the pan-European media landscape, by showing that of the channel's 20 million daily viewers, three million are in Europe's top 20% of income earners – reaffirming Eurosport's position as the strongest media brand across the continent.

www.eurosport.com

FALKE
ERGONOMIC SPORT SYSTEM

Background

Falke is one of Europe's leading sports clothing and lifestyle brands. Headquartered in Schmallenberg, Germany, the company has been managed by the Falke family for four generations. The current managing partners, cousins Paul Falke and Franz-Peter Falke are the great-grandsons of Franz Falke-Rohen, who founded a contract knitting mill in 1895.

After his death in 1928 his son, Franz Falke Jr continued to grow the company, expanding from yarn and stockings to outerwear. By the late 1960s, under the management of the third generation, Paul and Franz-Otto Falke, the company had become a major industrial enterprise, with a turnover of 100 million Euros. They focused on building the Falke brand name, investing in marketing and expanding Falke's export business, founding overseas production facilities in South Africa, Portugal, Austria and Hungary.

In 1990, following the death of Paul Falke, the company was taken over by his son Paul and the son of Franz-Otto, Franz-Peter Falke. Together, they now manage an international brand with a turnover of 185 million Euros.

The success of the Falke Group is based on its commitment to three principles: top quality, modern design and customer-oriented service.

Achievements

Falke has become one of Germany's best known brands, and one of its most successful exports. One of the company's product lines that has enjoyed particular success on the international market is the Falke Ergonomic Sports System. This is a range of socks and

Uncompromising demands of function, innovation, comfort and design

underwear specifically designed to meet the optimum performance requirements of the athlete. Using the principle of ergonomics, the system is the ultimate in hi-tech sports clothing.

The system adapts to the workings of the human body, using fabrics whose fit and material are fine-tuned to the wearer's anatomy. They also regulate temperature through moisture control, thermal insulation and cooling, and provide optimal protection and support for professional-standard sport.

The excellence of Falke's designs, developed in co-operation with internationally renowned biomechanics experts, such as the German Sports University of Cologne, is reflected in the top-level sportsmen and women who rely on Falke products. For example, Falke are outfitters to the German national Ski Team until the end of 2004 as well as the Austrian Ski Pool.

Product/Promotion

Falke Ergonomic Sports Socks are specifically designed for fourteen different types of sport: trekking, skiing, cross-country skiing, ski touring, snow-boarding, running, walking, tennis, biking, golf, cross-training, skating, fitness and motor biking. Each is packed with features designed to meet the requirements of that particular activity – for example the trekking socks protect against rain and stones, have quick-drying Coolmax fibres and provide optimal ankle protection.

Ski socks help reduce pressure on the shinbone, ankle and heel and there is even a sock, the SB1, specially designed for snowboarding.

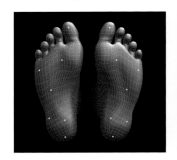

extremely good moisture transport through the use of a special material combination (pull - push technology)

optimum heat insulation through voluminous knitting technique

perfect air circulation through loose cut

optimum fit of the pants thanks to the customized use of Lycra zones

Falke Ergonomic Sport Underwear is produced with a circular knitting process, creating each item in one piece. On shirts there are no side seams at all, allowing the garment to stretch in all directions, giving the best-possible freedom of movement and avoiding friction and pressure points.

As with the range of sports socks, Falke Ergonomic Sports Underwear is designed around the three pillars of Anatomy, Climate Control and Support. Differentiated male and female fits, and optimal comfort and movement fits meet the Anatomy requirement of the underwear range, while Climate Control is satisfied using fabrics specially chosen for their controlled drying and thermal insulation properties, helping regulate the body temperature under diverse conditions. Support is catered for with designs that protect the muscular structure, and provide optimal movement control for all types of sport.

The range is divided into five categories. Ergonomic X-Treme is designed for activity at very low temperatures; Ergonomic Pro for

durable feel of freshness through the use of anti-bacterial silver ions

highly efficient cushioning effect through ergonomically adjusted cushions

perfect fit through asymmetrical toe (Left/Right) and anatomically shaped foot

optimum moisture transport and heat regulation through the use of high-tech yarns

activity at cool temperatures; Ergonomic Ultra for high levels of activity, Ergonomic Support, specifically designed to provide protection and support for women during sporting activity and the new Ultra Light, specifically for active sports in warmer temperatures.

In early 2004, Falke invested in a new marketing campaign for the Ergonomic Sports System, highlighting the emotion and colour of sport with high quality product shots and the strapline 'Form Follows You'. As with all other Falke advertising over the years, the company worked with internationally renowned photographers to create stunning high quality images that underline the premium quality of the Falke brand.

Falke sponsored the Karstadt Ruhr Marathon in 2003, which attracted nearly 2,000 participants. It also promotes the brand at sports events all over Europe, including the Paris and London marathons. Because of the technology that goes into making its garments, Falke is also regularly featured in the sports and technical press, making public relations an important promotional channel.

Falke's overall identity is based on tradition, performance and experience. With over 100 years in the business, there are few brands that have so consistently stood for innovation, quality and timeless modernity.

www.falke.com

FILA

Background

Established in 1911 in Biella, Italy, Fila began life in the textiles business before going on to specialise in knitwear production. After consolidating its expertise in the Italian textiles industry, the company only entered the world of sport clothing in 1973. The brand soon made an impact, especially in tennis with its famous cotton rib tubular knit design. The design was revolutionary, not only because it was manufactured using a tubular process not seen before in sportswear, but also because Fila's use of colour blocking brought about the demise of traditional tennis whites.

It was Bjorn Borg's elegance and grace, as well as his famous determination to be a champion, that brought the Fila brand to the attention of the world.

In 2003, Fila became a subsidiary of Sport Brands International (SBI), and under the direction of Steve Wynne (formerly President/CEO of adidas America Inc) the new global management team is reviewing all activities worldwide.

The company still has offices in Milan and a design, research and development facility in Montebelluna, Italy. Fila now also has global resources in New York and Sparks, Maryland.

Although it is an international brand, Fila has remained faithful to its Italian origins, with a commitment and a passion for sports and an inherent flair for creative design.

Achievements

Fila has a great tradition of supporting champions that have achieved legendary status in the world of sport. The list includes world-famous tennis stars Bjorn Borg, Boris Becker and Gabriele Sabatini, the golfer Tom Watson, the mountaineer Reinhold Messener, and the ski champions, Ingemar Stenmark and Alberto Tomba. All are athletes who have competed with passion and with style.

And that legacy continues today with tennis champions Jennifer Capriati, Kim Clijsters and the winners of the London and Boston Marathons, Robert Cheruyoit and Margaret Okayo.

Thanks to this longstanding support of leading athletes, as well as its sponsorship of world-class events, Fila has built a global reputation as an authentic and elite sport brand, committed to bringing innovation in design and performance to consumers around the world.

Product/Promotion

With more than 30 years experience in the world of sport, especially tennis, running, fitness and ski, Fila is an innovator in product design and technology.

Its design philosophy is influenced by its Italian heritage which is reflected in beautiful, authentic as well as functional sports products. The Fila brand is currently being revitalised through a redefined brand positioning, a new target audience, and an updated corporate identity.

Fila's future positioning will be driven by five guiding principles: 'Vero' (authentic sport); 'Audace' (bold, differentiation through risk-taking); 'Innovativo' (innovation); 'Elegante' (elegance) and 'Unitario' (unified as one company, one brand around the world).

> Born of Italian heritage, the Fila brand has a rich design tradition, steeped in form and function, grace and performance

www.fila.com

These principles will be exemplified in Fila's approach to designing sports footwear and clothing. In footwear, the brand has already developed technologies such as the Dynamic Landing System, which maximises transition smoothness for each type of foot, and Flow Technology, which absorbs shock, cradles the foot and helps 'guide' it through the gait as well as offering unique breathability properties.

Among the Fila range of tennis shoes is the X point II, engineered for the player who centres their game around speed. The shoe is stable, durable and very lightweight. For running, the Flow Reckoning Control shoe features Fila's dynamic landing system, as well as its proprietary Evergrip, Superaction and Evergrind features.

In clothing, Fila Performa is recognised as among the best in the category for its wickability and moisture resistance. All items made with Performa quickly transfer perspiration outside of workout gear so that it evaporates quickly. It also has an anti-bacterial treatment that helps protect against skin irritation and infection. Performa material is soft to the touch, elastic, lightweight and is used throughout Fila's performance collections.

Fila is extending its brand into two key areas: Vintage and Filativa. The Vintage ranges highlight Fila's design credentials and will be distributed through selected trend and independent retailers.

Filativa is a creative, Italian-designed casualwear category, inspired by Fila's core sport categories. Progressive, fun and fashionable – this range has been designed to appeal to a younger, value-driven market.

The brand gains valuable exposure via its support of world-class athletes, sports federations and sporting events. It has received high visibility through its sponsorship of the US Open, the Grand Slam tennis tournament staged in New York.

Fila will also continue to reach a massive audience through its sponsorship of the Italian Winter Sports Federation, ahead of key international events in Italy such as the 2006 Winter Olympics.

GRAYS
INTERNATIONAL

Background
From WG Grace to Brian Lara; the Rugby World Cup to the origins of hockey, one brand's powerful position remains undimmed as it approaches a significant anniversary.

In 2005, Grays will have been at the root of some of the best known sporting products for 150 years – a time frame which has seen its products used by sports stars who have long since assumed legendary status and provides the brand with a gravitas missing from many other modern day marques.

Founded in 1855 by World Rackets Champion HJ Gray, through growth and acquisition it today boasts a powerful portfolio of brand names familiar around the world.

Still under the control of the Grays family, the brand has been involved in businesses as diverse as soccer, snooker, sub-aqua, fishing tackle, bowls, toys, sports publishing, retailing and even building. Many have since disappeared but their heritage and legacy lives on and their unique strengths have been distilled into their descendants that are all household names today: Gray-Nicolls in cricket; Gilbert in rugby union; Grays in hockey and racket sports and Steeden in rugby league.

Achievements
With a desire to innovate and inspire, all four brands are constantly pushing back the boundaries as they seek to reinforce their market position.

Gray-Nicolls' ground-breaking developments over the years included the first covered bats, the first use of coloured labels, the first to introduce steel and later titanium sprung handles, the first shoulder-less bat and in 1974 the 'scoop' bat which revolutionised cricket bat manufacture by allowing redistribution of weight across the blade – and hence a larger sweet-spot for the first time. This technology has since been re-applied to create a series of successful derivates, culminating in the new Phoenix bat. More recently its bowed bat technology has resulted in the introduction of the Longbow and the Powerbow, the best selling bat of 2004.

Gilbert were supplying balls to Rugby School when the sport was invented there in 1823 and have remained at the forefront of the game ever since.

Having secured the use of its balls during the 1995 Rugby World Cup, Gilbert has operated a continuous programme of research and development to deliver a new superior performing ball for each World Cup. The new Xact ball selected for the 2003 tournament featured a totally new pimple pattern, 'Truflight' valve technology and distance with outstanding handling properties.

Grays' hockey sticks were the first to introduce reinforcement for durability and performance and laminated heads which enabled the unique 'hook' style head shape – and the first brand to replicate the playing qualities of wooden sticks with the new composite material technology. The new GX Turbo range of sticks developed in conjunction with sports leading players and leading material scientists are enjoying huge success.

Product/Promotion
A key part of the brand philosophy is to ensure its

> The Grays brand aims to be rated by players as the best on the field through innovation, product quality and in use at the highest levels of international sport

products are used on the world stage, a perfect sales platform around which much of its marketing activity revolves, mixed with the historic punch that only the makers of the cricket bat used by WG Grace to notch up his 100th century, can muster.

Today Gray-Nicolls has a 'world XI' of top names endorsing its range of bats.

Meanwhile, a deal with the Rugby World Cup and a host of competitions, both domestic and international, showcase the Gilbert brand, while the widespread use of its hockey sticks at the Athens Olympic Games provided it with unparalleled exposure.

Steeden is used exclusively in the Super League, Australian NFL and major internationals. Grays racquets have been used by more winners of the British Squash Open than any other brand and Australian Paul Price is the latest of a long line of internationals to use Grays racquets.

Since the 1980s Grays has successfully extended each of their brand's franchise to sport specific luggage, footwear, clothing and protection to enable the end user to identify with and benefit from the same brand values for all their playing needs.

A modern marketing strategy for a brand that still remains true to its roots from all those years ago.

www.grays-int.com

Harrows
DARTS TECHNOLOGY

Background

Harrows Darts Technology is the world's leading darts brand. Founded in 1973, when it started business from a small darts shop in Enfield, North London, Harrows now produces and stocks over 800 specialised products, which are sold by sport retailers and chain stores throughout the world.

The company was born out of a surge in popularity for darts when the sport was first televised in the 1970s. Tapping into the trend, Harrows seized the opportunity to capitalise on domestic UK demand and prepared for the anticipated expansion of the sport overseas.

Taking darts technology around the world

The early 1980s saw a concerted focus on developing export sales. Affiliating itself with emerging darts associations around the world, and also by sponsoring tournaments outside of the UK, Harrows built an early presence in countries which are now enthusiastically playing darts. Some 30 million players worldwide now take part in the sport.

In the mid 1980s, Harrows teamed up with Eric Bristow, the five times World Champion, five times World Master and undisputed 'name and face' of darts. This, the biggest player sponsorship deal of all time, was signed live on TV. It netted 'The Crafty Cockney' £250,000, but proved to be a pivotal deal for Harrows, dramatically increasing the profile of the company.

The company's factories and global headquarters are located in Hoddesdon, Hertfordshire, from where it controls all aspects of design, production and distribution, to over 95 countries.

Achievements

Over the years, Harrows has built itself into a great British success story, with a unique role in the worldwide sports trade.

It has helped transform the sport of darts, driving its appeal beyond the UK. Harrows' export sales now account for over 70% of its output, covering North America, every country in Continental Europe, Australasia and the Far East. Large volumes of stock are now even being shipped into China, where English-produced darts are held in high regard.

Harrows has gone to unprecedented lengths to spread the 'darts gospel', supporting the sport in the remotest of regions, such as the Solomon Islands, where it sponsors the official Darts League. One of Harrows' most far-flung adventures was to sponsor the Mongolian Open, in Ulan Bator. This tournament was unique. Instead of the usual

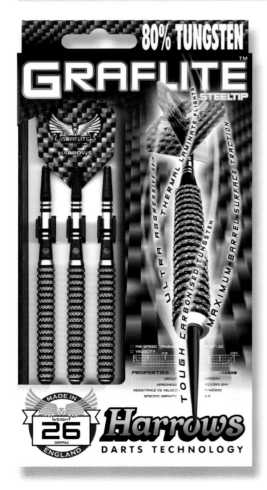

trophy, the tournament winner walked away with an unusual first prize – a horse.

With this international outlook, Harrows has proved that a sport with simple rules, relatively inexpensive equipment and little space required in which to play, can be introduced to almost any country.

Product/Promotion

Eric Bristow continues to promote the company's products in the print and broadcast media. Because Bristow was at the peak of his powers when darts was making its mark on TV, he remains an iconic figure for the sport and to this day is an effective figurehead for Harrows. The Bristow Legend lives on, and has become intertwined with the Harrows brand.

In addition to the Bristow endorsement, the company also sponsors up and coming players, both at home and overseas, helping nurture the stars of tomorrow.

Harrows originally marketed itself with the strapline of 'Pure Dartsmanship'. In 1985, it switched this to 'Darts Technology' – a line Harrows felt more clearly reflected its focus, which, from the outset, has always been on quality and innovation.

Point of purchase systems are an important promotional tool for Harrows, which was the first company to carve a distinct positioning for darts at retail. Prior to Harrows coming into the market, darts had no true retail 'home', being mixed in with assorted other sporting goods and often not being noticed by shoppers. To make them stand out, Harrows developed a range of point of sale merchandisers,

which could be sited to give a clear darts presence within a shop. The units are based around a modular packaging system that allows the stockist to pick and mix according to individual market needs.

Over the years, Harrows products have been at the leading edge of technical innovation. Amongst its ground-breaking products have been the Power Point Kinetic Energy System, which helps reduce darts 'bounce outs', Dimplex flights for increased strength and longer playing life, and ultra high density tungsten for a maximum weight to volume ratio.

All of this has seen Harrows play a vital role in enhancing darts' image from a traditionally blue collar pursuit, played in smoky British clubs and pubs, to a high-profile international sport.

www.harrows-darts.com

Background

There's no doubt that the Heineken Cup breaks new ground and is rugby's first cross border competition. The Heineken Cup allows the best to compete with the best and no less importantly gives supporters the opportunity to enjoy new cultures and begin friendly rivalries – there's intense competition and mutual respect. It is also swelling in popularity with pool weekend match attendance figures having risen year on year, from 20,000 in 1995 to 109,000 in 2004.

The Heineken Cup was launched in 1995. The idea of a pan-European club rugby tournament was the initiative of the Five Nations Committee – now the Six – to provide a new level of professional cross-border competition. This marked a new dawn for professional rugby in Europe and created one of sport's most exciting and prestigious annual competitions.

Twelve teams from Ireland, France, Wales, Italy and Romania took part in the first ever Heineken Cup of 1995-96. In the final, played in front of a 22,000-strong crowd at Cardiff Arms Park, the French team Toulouse required extra time before beating Cardiff 21-18 to become Champions of Europe.

While that first tournament consisted of just fifteen matches, England and Scotland joined the competition in 1996-97 to make it a truly European event.

Thanks to the determination of the body that organises it, ERC and to its title sponsor Heineken, the Heineken Cup soon took a grip on players and supporters. With 20 teams competing, the expanded second tournament drew even bigger crowds, with 41,664 turning out at Cardiff Arms Park, and a TV audience of millions, watched Brive destroy Leicester 28-9.

The following season, ERC introduced home and away fixtures in the pool rounds. This guaranteed each team a minimum of six games and created a bumper tournament of 70 matches. Bath were crowned European Champions that year, beating cup-holders Brive in a 19-18 thriller.

Achievements

In the Heineken Cup, ERC has given European rugby the prestigious tournament

it deserves. The increased professionalism of club rugby during the 1990s demanded an opportunity for teams to compete on an international stage. The Heineken Cup has not only met this challenge, it has enormously raised the profile and popularity of club rugby in the process.

As it celebrates its tenth anniversary in the 2004-05 competition, the Heineken Cup has quickly established itself as a premier sporting event.

The rising audiences, both at the turnstile and watching on television, are testament to the popularity of the tournament. The 22,000 that watched the first-ever final in 1996, swelled to 68,441 by 2000 and 73,000 in 2004.

During the 2004-2005 competition, the five-millionth fan will pass through the gates to watch a Heineken Cup match.

Every year, the Heineken Cup has served up more intense competition, more dedication from clubs and fans, and more excitement on the pitch. Wasps' victory over Toulouse in the 2004 final was widely hailed as the best of the nine finals in the history of the tournament.

Product/Promotion

Alongside the Heineken Cup, ERC also organises two other well-

> Progressive, transparent, dynamic and authoritative – much like the game itself

www.ercrugby.com

known rugby tournaments for professional club teams in Europe, the European Challenge Cup and the European Shield. However, it is the Heineken Cup, which is the jewel product in ERC's crown and the tournament with which the organisation is most closely identified.

ERC itself has invested heavily in its brand positioning and focus, hiring brand consultancy Interbrand to create a new identity in 2002. This helps it communicate its position as the professional, co-ordinating and dynamic face of Europe's premier rugby club competitions, putting it in the same frame of reference as brands such as UEFA and the PGA, no small achievement when you consider that the brand is a mere decade old.

ERC promotes its brand and competitions in a variety of ways, including its website www.ercrugby.com. The number of visitors to the site is growing rapidly, attracted by its in-depth coverage of European rugby, and a new development, the first-ever Heineken Cup Fantasy Rugby game. ERC also uses the internet to send out a highly regarded media newsletter, ERC.com News. This is mailed to 1,500 journalists every week, helping ERC get its brand and coverage of the Heineken Cup into the papers. Every year, ERC also sends out 3,000 copies of its authoritative Media Guide to journalists, providing squad details and statistics about every aspect of the Heineken Cup.

ERC also gains publicity from its exclusive annual ERC Elite Awards, honouring the clubs and players who have performed best in the Heineken Cup.

The winners read like a who's who of international rugby.

howies®

Background

Clothing company howies hails from Cardigan, a small town on the west coast of Wales. The unconventional 'HQ' reflects its quirky personality. The building is more reminiscent of a double garage than an international sports clothing operation. The staff use garden furniture and the warehouse has only recently been fitted with that most basic of storage devices – shelves.

However, although oddball, howies is one of the most influential sports brands in the UK.

It was started by David and Clare Hieatt in 1995, from their living room floor. They set out to create an active sports brand that made high quality, stylishly functional clothing for the sports they loved – mountain biking, skateboarding, snowboarding and the outdoors in general.

But more than that, they wanted the company to have an environmental and social conscience. The mission from day one was to run the company as a tool to make people think about the world they live in.

The company started off making t-shirts, boldly displaying some of these beliefs. They were an instant hit and were soon selling fast. The company is now

famous for this running social commentary. One of its most famous t-shirts called 'shoplifter', set off shop alarms with a little device planted in the sleeve. It was eventually withdrawn from sale after the police threatened action.

The company measures its success on how much debate, talk and discussion it creates. Getting bigger is not a concern, only getting better.

Achievements

The success of howies is that it has stayed true to its beliefs –

> Honesty, innovation, provocation, environmentalism, quality, passion and fun

come what may, even when it couldn't afford to.

It donates 1% of its turnover to environmental and social causes and is one of the biggest users of organic cotton in the UK. howies was one of the first to introduce organic cotton denim jeans, washed using an innovative environmentally-friendly 'eco ball'.

In 1999 Fashion Weekly placed howies ahead of Nike and adidas in a list of influential brands. howies has consistently been voted one of the top brands by mountain bikers and skateboarders as well as The Sunday Times heralding it as a key ethical brand.

Furthermore, in the influential 200% Cotton book on the world's best t-shirts, howies features more than almost any other brand.

The company is proud of the way it treats its employees, giving staff 'too nice to be here' days off and giving full pay for maternity leave to its female staff.

Thanks to initiatives like this, howies can partly attribute its success to the motivation and satisfaction of its staff. It's a fun place to work but also a challenging one. A doormat at the entrance reads: Average not welcome.

There are few rules at howies, but one is strictly adhered to: that all tea should be made in the pot.

Product/Promotion

Since the early days, howies has grown the clothing range to include technical clothing, like its multi award-winning superfine merino base layers. howies also makes snowboard jackets, manufactured from natural high density cotton, guaranteed to last fifteen years.

howies loves ideas. So far, some of its best include the world's first donor card t-shirt – legally binding if the wearer has an accident. The unique howies Bike Bag uses a road-sign as a safety device. And, in the pipeline, is a pair of surf shorts that change colour in polluted seawater, warning surfers that they may be in danger.

howies hates to follow. It wants to find better ways of doing things. It believes that if you make a jacket like everything else, you only make a jacket. If you make a jacket that is unique and better than what is out there, you make a difference.

The unorthodox howies catalogue is its main promotional tool. From a small pamphlet, it is now a 150 page mini book that comes out twice a year. This has quietly become a cult item. Instead of filling it with product shots, howies devotes half the pages to how it thinks.

howies cares not only about its message, but how it puts it across. It talks about info-tainment rather than preaching. Humour, irony, art,

www.howies.co.uk

graphics, music, books, film and, of course, the clothing all have a quirky, oddball voice. Ultimately, the people at howies believe people can learn more while laughing their heads off.

KOOKABURRA

Background

It could be argued that Kookaburra would be within its rights to patent the sound of leather on willow such is the pivotal role the brand has played in the evolution of cricket. With traditions as old as the sport itself, the Kookaburra cricket ball is presently used exclusively in all one day international cricket and 85% of Test cricket – a fine testament of trust in a brand that has matched step for step the sport's advancements over the last century.

As cricket has moved forward so has Kookaburra's range of products ensuring that the quality of the equipment being used consistently matched the improving standards being set on the pitch. This reputation for quality and innovation lies at the heart of the Kookaburra brand.

Kookaburra was established in 1890, the brainchild of saddle and harness maker Alfred Grace Thompson. After emigrating to Australia in search of a warmer climate, Thompson found that his trade was being eaten away by the advent of the motor industry and consequently decided to use his expertise in leather to expand into the provision of sporting goods. Ably assisted by his sons Bill and Alf, Thompson's traditional production methods were soon in demand, particularly within the burgeoning cricket ball market.

From these beginnings, the Kookaburra brand has been propelled forward by four generations of the Thompson family, all the while remaining true to the need for product development to remain at the core of the business.

Achievements

One of the primary developments that the brand has been responsible for is the creation of more efficient machines to produce the balls, gradually replacing the time consuming need for hand sewing while maintaining the improvement in quality of the end result.

It is not solely in its core competency of cricket balls that the Kookaburra brand has made an impact. In the mid 1980s the company diversified into the marketing of all areas of personal cricket equipment ranging from bats and protective wear to clothing and footwear.

Not a brand to rest on its laurels, product development continues apace with the use of high technology materials helping Kookaburra to launch a new cricket bat in 2004 that boasts increased levels of durability and performance. The pursuit of providing 'all that the cricketer needs' is an ethos that the company lives by.

Product/Promotion

Kookaburra has utilised endorsement deals to indicate the trust that international players have in the brand. The firm currently enjoys the backing of Australian Test skipper Ricky Ponting and potentially as much as 50% of the country's touring party to England for the 2005 Ashes series could be Kookaburra endorsees.

Internationally the endorsement list is as impressive with England's Graham Thorpe and Sri Lankan Sanath Jayasuriya among those using the brand.

The company presently has offices in the bulk of the world's cricket playing countries (Australia, the UK, South Africa, New Zealand, India and Pakistan) in addition to a number of distribution operations in various other regions.

Hockey is another sport where Kookaburra is leading the way with the brand's Dimple Elite ball now used exclusively in all international matches worldwide, and it has also been used as the official Olympic ball since 1984. The development of this plastic covered product to replace the previous leather ball was revolutionary considering the advent of artificial grass on hockey fields. Leather balls had been found to be unsuitable for use on this surface as they absorbed water that caused them to swell.

Production lines have not been limited to hockey balls with Kookaburra's durable Composite Sticks proving highly popular while the clothing range has received the endorsement of all the English national teams, thanks principally to the development of 'climate control' fabrics.

Not content with cornering the equipment market for these sports, Kookaburra is constantly working on new and expanding product lines for the likes of rugby, soccer and netball, helping to keep the Kookaburra name in front of the sporting public throughout the calendar year.

www.kooka.com.au

LORD'S
THE HOME OF CRICKET

Background

The most famous and historic cricket venue in the world, Lord's is universally recognised by those inside and outside the game as 'The Home of Cricket'. Originally established in 1814 by entrepreneur Thomas Lord, the thirteen-acre site in North West London is steeped in nearly 200 years of cricket history.

The venue started life as the third home of Marylebone Cricket Club (MCC). As cricket has evolved, the Ground has subsequently become the headquarters of Middlesex County Cricket Club, the England and Wales Cricket Board and the world governing body, the International Cricket Council. The Ground itself has grown over the years to a capacity of up to 30,000, while the site also boasts an array of conference and leisure facilities. The Ground may have evolved as the times

have demanded, in particular with the introduction of the futuristic NatWest Media Centre in April 1999, but its heart has remained untouched, preserving its great heritage. The Members' Pavilion, built in 1890, is the oldest building at Lord's, containing the famous Long Room through which players make their way to and from the wicket.

Achievements

On the pitch, many of cricket's most memorable moments have occurred at Lord's, notably, in 1884, when the venue played host to its first ever Test Match, when England defeated Australia by an innings. Lord's may be steeped in the traditions of the game but the Ground has also been at the forefront of developments off the field. In 1938, Lord's became the first Ground to introduce TV cameras for a Test Match, now a prerequisite of any international sporting arena. The erection of the NatWest Media Centre, one of the leading facilities of its kind, also pays testament to the Ground's continual evolution.

The Home of Cricket

As well as having an unsurpassed view of the action, the Centre provides the world's media with the latest technological advancements. Even as recently as this year, new ground has been broken with the introduction of a see-through sightscreen in front of the Pavilion. The opening of the new Indoor Cricket School in 1995 indicates that Lord's has acknowledged the need to provide leading training facilities for cricketers. Further additions – such as conference rooms, corporate hospitality offerings, a Museum and Library, and the Lord's Tour – combine to create the year-round experience that Lord's offers today.

Product/Promotion

Historically, Lord's has used its traditions and place in cricket folklore as a platform to provide exposure and brand-building opportunities for its array of commercial partners. Vehicles such as perimeter board advertising, corporate hospitality, and match day promotions have all been used by the Ground to promote its partnering brands.

In May 2002, a decision was taken by MCC to increase the public-facing presence and identity of the Lord's brand itself.

With the aim of attracting new and broader audiences to the Ground, branding consultancy Cognosis was hired to help create a short-, mid- and long-term action plan to enhance the Lord's proposition. The strategy is not just about attracting fans to the Ground but also creating a welcoming and clearly defined brand experience for them whilst they are there. In line with this, a new logo identity was introduced and an elite group of top tier sponsors – The Lord's Partner Programme

– was established. The Ground's array of facilities have also been marketed more aggressively while subtle marketing promotions have been used to make the Lord's brand more visible on-site. Central to all the marketing activity that Lord's undertakes is the Ground's justified claim to be 'The Home of Cricket' – a mantra that clarifies the brand's status within the game.

www.lords.org

LTA
TENNIS NATION

Background

As the governing body of British tennis, the LTA is committed to growing the sport throughout the country at all levels; from the grass roots to success on the international stage. It works with clubs, schools, local authorities and other tennis federations to make tennis accessible, affordable and attractive. Ultimately, its success is judged not only by the number of people playing tennis in Britain, but the standard at which they play.

The LTA traces back to 1873, when the game of lawn tennis was invented by the Englishman, Major Walter Wingfield. The Championships at Wimbledon were first played in 1877, leading to the foundation of the LTA itself in 1888, with William Renshaw, six times Wimbledon Champion, becoming the first President.

In 1920 and 1922, formal agreements were signed with the All England Club for the management of the Lawn Tennis Championships and in 1934 a joint committee was formed between the LTA and the AELTC to manage The Championships.

As part of the drive to improve Britain's prospects as a tennis playing nation, in 2004 the LTA unveiled plans for a new National Tennis Centre (NTC) to be based at Roehampton. Opening in late 2006 the NTC will have world-class facilities, creating a high performance environment for top British players of every age.

Achievements

From its foundations as a volunteer association, the LTA has evolved into a progressive, effective and business orientated organisation.

> Driven by its vision to make Britain a great tennis nation and its mission for more players, better players

Working closely with the Government and Sport England it secured Government funding for the first time ever in 2004, and is striving to help nurture more and better tennis players for Britain. After a programme of modernisation working with external specialist consultants, it is now one of the most progressive sports governing bodies.

The LTA has launched dynamic, forward-thinking initiatives, such as City Tennis Clubs. CTCs are a new wave of public clubs, breathing life into

LTA

neglected and often unused inner city courts. This is a much-needed force for cultural change in British tennis, designed to bring the sport to kids who may never have had the chance to play, at a price they can afford.

The LTA has enlisted high-profile support for the scheme. Prime Minister Tony Blair is an official ambassador, while other sporting stars lending their support include John McEnroe, Venus Williams, Boris Becker and Ian Wright. Such support has helped CTCs gain valuable media coverage, worth over £22 million in the last three years.

In working further to shift the image of the game, the LTA also encourages young people to play through its Play Tennis campaign, backed by Tim Henman. This grass roots promotion is designed to encourage all people to try their hand at the game for free and 'Do More Than Just Watch'.

In 2004, it was supported by a nine-month media campaign and attracted press coverage worth £7 million. In 2004, the LTA's Play Tennis programme was nominated in the Sports Industry Awards for Best Promotion of a Sport by a Governing Body. The CTC

programme was also nominated, for Best Use of PR in a Sport Campaign.

Product/Promotion

In addition to the flagship brand, the LTA has created a range of sub-brands, designed to target specific segments. The idea is to make tennis relevant for different ages and lifestyles and to attract new kids into the sport and extend the profile beyond the Wimbledon fortnight.

Mini Tennis is the LTA's product for engaging 4-10 year-olds in the game. Introduced in 2001, over 700 clubs and 70,000 children now play Mini Tennis across Britain. This programme is designed to make tennis fun, accessible and rewarding.

For older kids, the LTA is introducing another sub-brand, RAW Tennis. This is designed to keep tennis interesting and aspirational for teenagers who have so many other activities to tempt them. Also designed to provide them with a clear pathway to progress, RAW Tennis will be launched nationally in early 2005.

At a professional level, the LTA's flagship events are Wimbledon (run in partnership with the AELTC), the Stella

Artois Championships and a number of other WTA and ATP tour events. The LTA also stages domestic events and administers all teams that represent Great Britain, ranging from the Davis Cup team to junior national teams and Great Britain's world-class wheelchair teams.

This strategy of sub-brands are united under the LTA master brand, which uses the strapline 'Tennis Nation' to encapsulate its mission to nurture and enhance British tennis.

The LTA's professionalism and the strength of its brand has attracted corporate partners and consumer brands who are helping to improve the image of tennis through marketing and effective communications. For example as a committed sponsor of the LTA, Ariel recently ran a cause related campaign to help identify tennis champions of the future, giving away free tennis lessons with ads on four million packs of washing powder.

Background

Founded in 1787, Marylebone Cricket Club (MCC) quickly established a reputation as the foremost Cricket Club in London, and subsequently became guardian of the Laws of the game. The first code of the Laws issued by the Club dates from around 1790,

settled at its third home in St. John's Wood, North West London, in 1814. Named after Thomas Lord, the man who found it on behalf of the Club, the famed Lord's Ground has been home to MCC ever since. From these roots, MCC has grown into the best-known international Cricket Club with over 18,000 members. Of these, over 1,500 are active playing members, giving MCC the largest playing membership of any Cricket Club in the world. To service this membership, the Club plays more than 400 matches in a typical season, both in the UK and abroad. The Club's women Members (incorporated in 1999) also enjoy a growing fixture list. With a commitment to promoting cricket worldwide, MCC operates globally and locally with equal fervour.

The matches hosted at Lord's between England and national touring sides are the highest-profile activities with which MCC is associated. The Club's jurisdiction over the Laws of the game ensures that MCC's influence is present wherever in the world there is cricket being played, be it a Test Match or a domestic club game. MCC has been responsible for numerous enhancements to technique, equipment and even audience expectations over the years and reviews the Laws regularly, managing debate on which developments should be incorporated to enhance and enrich the game.

MCC was also heavily active in the creation of the structural governance of the game in the UK as it is today. Since MCC was a private club, however, it could not receive public funds, so it set up a number of cricketing councils and governing bodies to administer

detailing the 22 yards between the wickets and the various ways that players could be given out. These Laws were subsequently adopted throughout the game and, to this day, MCC remains the custodian and arbiter of the Laws which govern cricket around the world.

After short stays at Dorset Fields in Marylebone and North Bank in Regent's Park, MCC

Achievements

Cricket was initially considered a sport for the elite. MCC was largely responsible for opening up the game to the masses, both domestically and internationally, from its early involvement in County Cricket in the 1870s through to its undertaking of official responsibility for the first England tour to Australia in 1903.

Owner of Lord's and Guardian of the Laws of Cricket

the professional game. These domestic bodies, now unified under the banner of the England and Wales Cricket Board, receive financial help from the government as a result. The Club also plays a pivotal role in identifying young players and nurturing them into future stars – the MCC Young Cricketers Scheme is one of the leading academies of its type.

Product/Promotion

MCC's principal role has been to promote and protect cricket's rules and regulations, and perhaps most importantly safeguard the 'spirit of the game'. To this end, the Laws of Cricket include a written statement addressing the 'Spirit of the Game'. The statement emphasises the importance of fair play and mutual respect between competing teams and MCC has introduced numerous initiatives to ensure that this message is received and understood by all who play the game throughout the world.

As well as its domestic programme, MCC's service to cricket has an international reach. Up to ten overseas playing tours are organised each year with a view to increasing the international appeal of cricket both in countries where it is well-established and where it is in the developmental stages.

MILLENNIUM STADIUM
CARDIFF ARMS PARK

STADIWM Y MILENIWM
PARC YR ARFAU CAERDYDD

The Millennium Stadium redevelopment option eventually chosen and supported by the Millennium Commission became the fourth redevelopment in the history of the Cardiff Arms Park site.

Today only the shell of the old North Stand of Cardiff Arms Park remains, incorporated into the state-of-the-art new facility. In its place is a venue capable of holding 73,434 people at capacity, all seated.

The stadium's trademark 8,000 tonne retractable roof adds drama to this awe-inspiring structure. It is carried by more than 4,700 wires and has a total length of 150 miles. This is the first of its kind in the UK and is instantly recognisable, towering above the Cardiff skyline.

Background

Constructed on the site of the world famous Cardiff Arms Park rugby stadium, the Millennium Stadium has continued to build on the site's rich heritage as a sporting venue. The first sports played there date back to 1848, with the first organised rugby union match taking place in 1874.

Five years prior to the stadium's final completion, a group redevelopment committee was set up to look at redeveloping the Wales National Stadium. In 1995, the WRU won the right to host the 1999 Rugby World Cup against severe competition from the Southern Hemisphere and the project came to life.

A review of the National Stadium at Cardiff Arms Park (designed in 1962) showed that it had long since been overtaken; with Twickenham and Scotland having developed stadia with capacities of 75,000 and 67,000 respectively and France about to build the Stade de France with a capacity of over 80,000.

A number of different development options were considered. One included adding a third tier to the existing Stadium, another suggested moving to a completely new site.

With the first retractable roof in the UK, the stadium is a multi-purpose, all round venue

IMAGES © WALES TOURIST BOARD

Achievements

In just five years, Cardiff's Millennium Stadium has become recognised around the world as one of the largest, multi-functional venues.

Since its opening in June 1999, it has welcomed over 1.3 million visitors per year, earned the top five-star rating from European soccer governing body UEFA, and has hosted a range of sports and entertainment events ranging from the Rugby World Cup final to sell-out concerts by the likes of Robbie Williams and the Red Hot Chilli Peppers. In addition, it is now the home of top events from such recognised organisations as the Welsh Rugby Union, the Football Association, the Football League, the Rugby Football League, the Football Association of Wales as well as the British Speedway Association.

The Millennium Stadium has witnessed some of the greatest recent moments in UK and international sport and, from the start, started smashing records. The Rugby World Cup final in 1999 recorded the first £5 million gate in the history of sport in the UK.

It also became part of the history of the world's most famous domestic football club competition 'the FA Cup' when the

Football Association chose it to host its showcase events. It became a true home for England's national game when the Football League joined the party bringing the League Cup and the Football League play-offs to the stadium, while work took place on the new Wembley Stadium.

On the eve of the new millennium it set a European indoor crowd record, when 50,000 revellers attended the first concert at the venue as Wales' leading band, the Manic Street Preachers, performed under a closed roof.

The Millennium Stadium is also on the list of proposed football venues in the bid submitted by London in its race to host the 2012 Olympic Games.

Product/Promotion

When most of the events staged at the stadium sell themselves, the marketing team at the Millennium Stadium continue to push back the boundaries of commercial strategies as they look to reinforce the brand image.

A particular recent focus has been on growing its corporate hospitality sales. The market has experienced considerable growth over the past twelve months, and the venue is looking to turn the sector into a £4 million-plus per annum business over the next few years.

It recently highlighted its hospitality offerings at a charity auction before the Arsenal vs Manchester United FA Community Shield – the curtain raiser to the 2004/5 season. Several new strategies were unveiled, including an 'annual licence fee' to secure seats for all the major sporting events and special packages for corporates to block book for particular events, such as Wales' FIFA World Cup 2006 qualifying campaign and the Lloyds TSB Autumn Series rugby union events.

Its commercial team know that to be successful it must put the needs of the customer first; a lesson learned during its early years. It therefore made club seats and hospitality box packages a lot simpler, improved the quality, and reduced its rates.

It hopes to score the sort of goals in the commercial department as it witnesses on the pitch as it continues to assist the Welsh economy with its big crowds and big ideas.

www.millenniumstadium.com

mitre ®

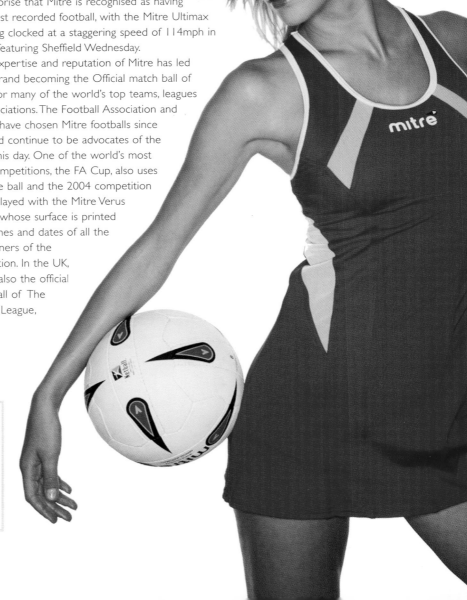

Background

Mitre has been part of British football heritage since its inception in the 1880s and is credited as being one of the original manufacturers of the first ever footballs. In reality the brand started about 60 years before this in 1817 when Ben Crook and his family started their small leather tannery business in Huddersfield, England. They produced only the finest quality leather products, and it is this passion and commitment to outstanding product that has ensured that Mitre has remained a leading British sports brand for almost 200 years, while many others have come and gone.

Achievements

It is on the football pitch where Mitre is most widely recognised and it's the range of iconic Mitre footballs that people think of first. Mitre are known throughout the World as the football experts.

Mitre Footballs are used at the very highest levels of the professional game, and amazingly each and every one of its pro footballs are still individually hand stitched and are crafted with such precision that each

ball is created to within just 3g of the ball's ideal weight and to within just 1mm of its perfect circumference. Any ball produced outside of these parameters does not make the pitch.

In addition to the simple production brilliance, the ball is rigorously and continuously aerodynamically tested and refined to deliver the ultimate match ball performance. It is the dedication to perfection that consistently sets Mitre apart from the competition and it's little surprise that Mitre is recognised as having the fastest recorded football, with the Mitre Ultimax ball being clocked at a staggering speed of 114mph in a game featuring Sheffield Wednesday.

The expertise and reputation of Mitre has led to the brand becoming the Official match ball of choice for many of the world's top teams, leagues and associations. The Football Association and England have chosen Mitre footballs since 1966 and continue to be advocates of the ball to this day. One of the world's most loved competitions, the FA Cup, also uses the Mitre ball and the 2004 competition will be played with the Mitre Verus football, whose surface is printed with names and dates of all the past winners of the competition. In the UK, Mitre is also the official match ball of The Football League,

At some point in your sporting career you are likely to have worn, kicked or touched Mitre

The Scottish Premier League, and Wales. Across Europe, Mitre is the official ball of The Greek Premier League, the Hungarian Football League and various pro clubs in Italy.

Product/Promotion

But for Mitre there is more to the beautiful game than just the professionals. Mitre has a ball to suit every age, pitch, player and standard. As experts, Mitre firmly believes in providing the very best product to each player, be it the beginner or the Sunday league player who continues to play way past his best days. Concepts such as Soccer Lite, Mini Soccer, Soft Touch and the Brazillian skill game Futebol de Salao will help maintain a stream of outstanding footballing talent for many years to come.

In addition to just footballs, Mitre also produces some top football boots. In 1998 Mitre developed SPEEDSTUD, a revolutionary stud design that is proven to increase drive and acceleration by up to 40% more than a traditional round stud design. In a game where speed is vital, such improvements are mind blowing, and to be able to get to the ball quicker and get ahead of your opponent, are key factors in changing the way the game is played.

More recently the brand has expanded into both rugby and netball. Mitre has an excellent pedigree on the rugby field, with the

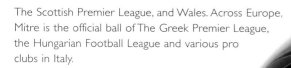

Mitre rugby ball used for the first ever Rugby World Cup. In 2001 Mitre transformed the rugby ball market and launched G-Spin, a rugby ball with grooved panels that allows kickers to curl the ball like their footballing friends – used for the first time in the Six Nations game between Italy and England.

Netball is still the most popular female sport in the UK and Commonwealth countries, with over eight million ladies playing worldwide and Mitre is one of the leading brands in World Netball.

In 2004 Mitre introduced a new kit collection designed in collaboration with leading women's fashion designer Madeleine Press. The sleek, stylish, figure hugging

www.mitre.com

performance dresses were well received and were awarded Best Designed Sports Kit of the Year 2004, proving Mitre is not only at the centre of the action on the pitch.

Nothing feels like a Mizuno

Background

The Mizuno company was founded by Rihachi Mizuno in 1906 as a family run sporting goods store in Osaka, Japan. Working with his younger brother Rizo, the Mizuno store specialised in the supply of baseball and golf equipment imported from the US.

After a while, Rihachi Mizuno became frustrated with the quality of imported products and sought local Japanese factories to manufacture to higher specifications. The domestic-made products were labelled under the family name, giving birth to the Mizuno brand.

In 1935 Mizuno opened its first sales headquarters in Osaka. 'Yodoyabashi' was the tallest building in its area and became a symbol of Mizuno's rising influence. The site remains special, as the building has been converted into Mizuno's flagship store at the heart of the city that grew around it.

The company's unique family management has always placed

great emphasis on the technical sophistication of their product, investing heavily in research, design and development. It was thanks to this that the performance of Mizuno's equipment came to the attention of the US and Europe's leading sportsmen and women. Mizuno's popularity amongst these sporting icons initiated the export of Mizuno products and the start of Mizuno's global business. The company is now a global force in the sports equipment market, with offices in Tokyo, Paris, Munich, Atlanta, Shanghai, Hong Kong and London.

Achievements

Mizuno now has a permanent place in sporting history. Carl Lewis, Ivan Lendl, Severiano Ballesteros, Nick Faldo, Rivaldo, and the New Zealand All Blacks all reached the pinnacle of their sports with Mizuno equipment.

It was in 1977 that Seve Ballesteros first played with Mizuno golf products on the Japanese Tour. Since then, Ballasteros and more of the game's greatest players have triumphed using Mizuno equipment. In addition, Nick Faldo has achieved triple victories in both the US Masters and the British Open using

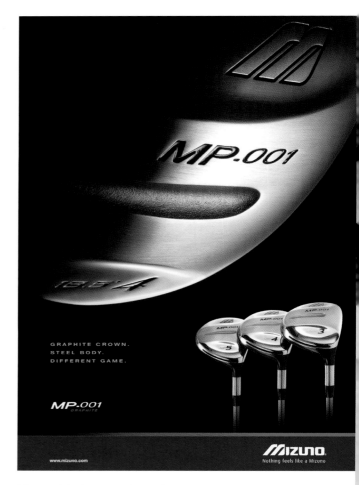

MP.001

GRAPHITE CROWN.
STEEL BODY.
DIFFERENT GAME.

MP.001
GRAPHITE

www.mizuno.com

Nothing feels like a Mizuno

Mizuno clubs. Success such as this has earned Mizuno a formidable reputation in world golf. By 1997, Mizuno irons were the most played brand by professional golfers on both the European and the US Professional Golf Tours. Most recently, Luke Donald completed a historic hat trick of wins for Mizuno irons, with victory at the Scandinavian Masters. Competing with his MP-33s, Donald's win was the third in a row for Mizuno irons on the PGA European Tour, following success at The Open Championship and the Irish Open.

So influential has Mizuno become in golf that it runs the official workshop for the PGA European Tour in golf and in Japan, it hosts The Mizuno Open, which has become one of the world's most prestigious golf tournaments.

> The brand aims to contribute to society through the advancement of sports and quality goods

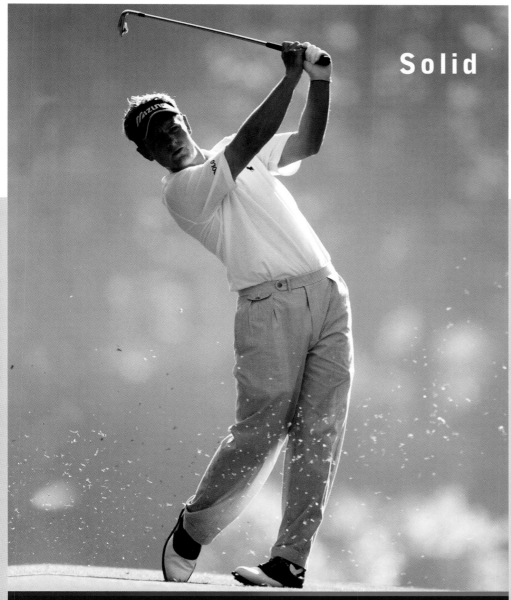

Solid

LUKE DONALD
MP-33 Grain Flow Forged irons, Dynamic Gold S300 steel shafts,
standard length, 1 degree upright, Tour Velvet cord grip, 58 round with single tape.
Visit www.mizuno.com for your local Mizuno Fitting Centre.

MIZUNO®
Nothing feels like a Mizuno

Mizuno has been a keen supporter of the Olympics since 1964 when it became an official supplier of the Tokyo Olympic Games. Some of the world's best athletes have competed and won at the highest level with the help of Mizuno. At the Barcelona Olympic Games in 1992, athletes using Mizuno products won a total of 72 medals.

Product/Promotion

After 100 years Mizuno's core beliefs remained much unchanged. Persistence with precision manufacturing and a preference for performance over fashion.

Mizuno makes a wide range of sports clothing, footwear and equipment using cutting-edge technology. For example, Mizuno's unique Grain Flow Forging process upholds this tradition as it is designed to maintain and strengthen the natural grain found in

quality steel. The process has been developed over many years at its exclusive forging factory in Hiroshima, Japan. Grain Flow Forging exceeds the conventional forging process by repeating the high pressure compression process to ensure a tight, uniform grain structure through the club head.

The quality and precision of the manufacturing process is reflected in the 'Nothing Feels Like a Mizuno' strapline that positions Mizuno forged irons as

offering a competitive advantage in the golf marketplace.

For its running shoes, Mizuno has developed Mizuno Wave, a new-function shoe with enhanced steadiness and cushioning. This is the only technology that combines the two essential properties needed in functional running footwear, cushioning and stability. A specially designed 'wave plate' cushions the foot by dispersing the force of impact across a larger surface area. It provides added stability thanks to the construction differing between the outside and the inside of the shoe, thereby protecting the midsole in high pressure areas.

Mizuno uses sponsorship as an important promotional tool, underlining the credibility of the brand by highlighting its use by leading athletes. Some of the elite athletes sponsored by Mizuno include the 1999 World Footballer of the Year, the Brazilian legend Rivaldo. Mizuno also sponsors the Namibian Commonwealth Games 200m Champion Frankie Fredericks, the Czech javelin world record holder and three time Olympic Champion Jan Zelezny, the 1996 Olympic Champions Dutch Volleyball Team, and the Australian Rugby Team.

www.mizuno.co.uk

Background

With 55 years of history, MotoGP is the pinnacle of motorcycle racing and the oldest of all motorsports World Championships.
First staged in 1949 by the Fédération Internationale de Motocyclisme, the competition has historically been known as the FIM World Championship, including different racing categories.

In 2002, the competition was revamped when a rule change allowed prototype bikes with four-stroke engines and up to 990cc capacity to compete in the premier class. These modifications have transformed the competition, with larger audiences and more excitement surrounding MotoGP than ever before.

It is now a truly global sports show, with the calendar for 2005 including seventeen Grand Prix during a nine month season to be held across five continents, in countries including Malaysia, South Africa, Australia, Qatar, Germany, Japan and the new entries of China and the US.

Achievements

MotoGP has gone from strength to strength since the rule change allowing more powerful bikes to compete in 2002. It is now the undisputed elite category of motorcycle racing, with the world's leading manufacturers – including Honda, Yamaha, Suzuki, Ducati,

Aprilia and Kawasaki – embracing the class. They now produce specially designed prototypes for MotoGP which are the most powerful machines in two-wheeled sport, with more than 240 horsepower and capable of top speeds of 340km/h.

MotoGP's position at the leading edge of motorcycle racing has attracted the most highly skilled technicians and the best riders in the world. The 25 year-old Italian Valentino Rossi is the superstar of the current generation of riders, winning five titles in the last eight years. For the 2004 season, he shocked the motorcycle world by switching from Honda to Yamaha. Other big names competing for the coveted prize of World Champion include Sete Gibernau, Max Biaggi, Alex Barros, Troy Bayliss, Colin Edwards, Neil Hodgson

and Kenny Roberts, all following in the footsteps of legendary riders such as Mick Doohan, Giacomo Agostini, Mike Hailwood or Barry Sheene.

Names like this and the excitement they generate has supercharged the popularity of MotoGP. In 2003, over 1.75 million people attended the sixteen Grand Prix. The biggest crowds of last year saw 204,000 turning out for the Grand Prix weekend at Germany's Sachsenring, and 203,000 in Jerez, Spain. The British round, at Donington Park, is amongst the most popular races, with over 82,000 spectators attending the event in 2004 on race-day alone.

Television audiences are also growing fast, with an average worldwide TV audience of 319 million watching coverage of each race in 2003. The event attracts over 3,500 hours of broadcast coverage every season, reaching 208 countries, of which 185 receive live coverage of races. Over 50 TV networks show live broadcasts of MotoGP. Swelling audiences are prompting some of these, including RTL in Germany, Mediaset in Italy, TVE in Spain and the BBC in the UK, to increase their coverage.

Broadcast technology conveys the excitement and atmosphere

of the competition. At every Grand Prix, there are over 20 trackside cameras, as well as 30 micro-cameras mounted on the bikes, radio frequency camera crews in the pit lanes and overhead cameras on helicopters.

MotoGP's official website, www.motogp.com, has seen a huge leap in traffic too, receiving 34 million visits in 2003, with registered subscribers from all around the world logging on to one of its eight language versions.

The worldwide attraction, extensive TV coverage, style and prestige of MotoGP has helped it attract a host of commercial partners and sponsors. From fashion to telecommunications and from drinks to cigarettes, MotoGP has become an attractive commercial property for the world's biggest brands, including Marlboro, Red Bull, Tissot, BMW, Dunlop, Cinzano, Veltins and Telefonica.

Product/Promotion

MotoGP should not be confused with the Superbike Championships, which feature production motorcycles modified for racing. MotoGP, with its specially designed prototype bikes, is a very different competition.

The World Championship is structured into three Grand Prix categories, each defined by the engine capacity of bikes that can participate: 125, 250 and MotoGP. Approximately 24 riders enter each MotoGP race, while the smaller 125 and 250 categories – which provide a stepping stone to the premier class – line up around 30 competitors.

As its growing popularity and global audiences have increased, MotoGP has become a powerful brand in its own right, standing for excitement, action, innovation, skill, youth, cutting edge technology and international appeal. All of this has helped the brand become a hot licensing property. MotoGP branded products, such as clothing, motorcycle gear, watches and toys can be bought all over the world, as well as MotoGP games for all platforms, including PS2, X-Box and 3G mobile phones.

> Excitement, action, innovation and skill using cutting edge technology

www.motogp.com

NEXT GENERATION
clubs

Background

David Lloyd was one of the UK's best known and most highly regarded tennis players, and following his retirement from a distinguished tournament career, he successfully applied his talents to business. After four years of research, business planning and raising financial backing, Lloyd opened his first indoor court club in Heston, West London. The David Lloyd Club Heston became a blueprint for a new network of clubs that played an important part in modernising British tennis. The Slater Tennis Foundation, the highly successful independent tennis academy which helped forge the career of Tim Henman,

was part of the David Lloyd Club model.

In spring 1992, Lloyd secured a highly publicised public listing for David Lloyd Clubs, a feat which helped him become Coopers & Lybrand Entrepreneur of the Year in 1994. In the same year, Lloyd was appointed Captain of the British Davis Cup tennis team.

When David Lloyd Leisure was sold to Whitbread plc in 1996, Lloyd and his son Scott decided to further expand the racquet and health club model. Scott Lloyd embarked on a finance raising campaign which saw him secure £23 million of private equity which he used to launch a new venture,

Next Generation Clubs. David Lloyd is still involved in the business, as a non-executive director.

Achievements

Next Generation Clubs has always set out to challenge the 'gym' mould. Instead, the concept of the clubs aims to embody all aspects of people's leisure time, taking the fitness and leisure concept a step further to focus more on health, lifestyle and well-being.

Each club incorporates a hair and beauty salon, spa, restaurant, bar and, in a new development, hotel facilities. Next Generation Club Dudley has ten luxurious en-suite rooms and the company's latest project, Next Generation Hatfield, which will be Europe's largest leisure, health and fitness club, will provide 23.

Next Generation Clubs has also made some important innovations in its gym product. Malcolm McPhail, director of health and fitness, pioneered the introduction of kids gyms to the UK through Next Generation Clubs. He has also developed specific youth training programmes for children from the age of two onwards through the Nova Programme, based on Scandinavian research.

Product/Promotion

The name 'Next Generation' makes reference to Scott Lloyd taking over the reins from his father David and being the next in line to take the club concept forward.

The Next Generation 'product' itself currently consists of eleven tennis, racquet and health clubs throughout the UK, together with further clubs in Adelaide, Sydney and Perth in Australia.

Next Generation Clubs strive to become part of members' lifestyles by offering more than just a gym. Instead, the clubs are the epitome of the modern day 'country club' with varied and extensive facilities to suit every type of member. Whether it is poolside

Aiming to be the best family-friendly Racquets, Health and Fitness Clubs in the UK and Australia

barbeques in the summer, crèche facilities or parties for members, Next Generation Clubs offer facilities and services that create an emotional buy-in and strengthen the relationship with members.

Each club averages 115,000ft² in size and generally includes; indoor and outdoor pools, whirlpool spas, indoor and outdoor tennis courts, squash and badminton courts, gymnasium, aerobic studio, outdoor aerobic studio, hair and beauty salon, restaurant, bar and business centre. There are also child-free 'Celsius' areas, with whirlpool spa, steam room and sauna.

For families, Next Generation Clubs offers extensive supervised children's activities under the 'Nova' umbrella, featuring indoor and outdoor splash pools, interactive play areas, aerobic classes and children's gym.

www.nextgenerationclubs.co.uk

Building on the success of the Slater Tennis Academy, Scott and David Lloyd are continuing their commitment to fostering new British tennis talent, by operating the David Lloyd Tennis Academy. Open to children up to the age of 13, the David Lloyd Tennis Academy is a natural extension of the Next Generation Club brand, sharing the same qualities of independence, innovation, education, expertise and excellence.

Next Generation Clubs are primarily a facility that is geared towards the family and this is reflected in all branded materials and marketing initiatives.

Promotion is undertaken at a local level using local radio or publications, giving readers and listeners one day passes to the club and the opportunity to win a years membership. Brand awareness is maintained by an ongoing public relations campaign targeting national, trade and regional press. Unique aspects of the clubs facilities are promoted, as is the expertise and knowledge of staff through editorial focusing on topics related to lifestyle, health and fitness.

Background

The roots of Nike lie on a running track at the University of Oregon, which is where the two founders Bill Bowerman and Phil Knight first met. Bowerman was the university's running coach and was renowned for building an unrivalled track and field programme. He taught his athletes to seek competitive advantage everywhere – in their bodies, their gear and their passion.

Phil Knight was a University of Oregon accounting student and a middle-distance runner under Bowerman. In 1962 Knight had this

idea about bringing athletic shoes from Japan to dislodge German domination in the US athletic footwear industry. That same year they formed the company Blue Ribbon Sports, they each invested US$500, shook hands and started importing.

In 1971, it was renamed Nike (after the Greek Goddess of Victory). After the mid 1980s, Nike entered a new era of success when it collaborated with basketball star, Michael Jordan. His first signature shoe, the Air Jordan, gained legendary status. In 1987 'Visible Air' was launched in a groundbreaking commercial set to the Beatles' song 'Revolution'.

To bring inspiration and innovation to every athlete* in the world.
*If you have a body, you are an athlete

eyewear, bags and socks, there remains a passionate focus for design innovation and functionality to support an athlete's performance.

Nike is famous for linking its brand to the performance of the world's top athletes. The company does not just sign athletes as mobile posters but uses their insights to constantly strive to improve footwear and apparel technology.

Although Nike is best known for its immortal line 'Just do it', the brand does not have a single manicured proposition. Over time, Nike has delivered a wide variety of messages and exposed a number of different aspects of its personality. This is true to the athletic experience, and keeps the brand fresh.

www.nike.com

Nike's support of the world's most popular sport – football, really helped to fuel the company's global appeal and the Nike brand is now associated with many of the world's best teams and players.

Further growth was aided by expansion into golf. Nike began to work with Tiger Woods in 1996 – the year before he won the US Masters by twelve strokes.

Achievements

Nike is now a US$12 billion company and the world's largest Sport and Fitness Company. The Nike 'Swoosh',

originally designed for a fee of US$35, is now one of the world's most recognised brands.

Product/Promotion

Nike's product goal is simple – enhance athletic performance. That goal has led to some impressive innovations.

Some of the company's early groundbreaking inventions include the 'Waffle' outsole (inspired by pouring rubber onto a waffle iron). Nike Air was the first air technology developed at Nike and it changed the way we think about cushioning. It remains the standard impact protection more than 20 years after its debut.

In 2001, Nike introduced another cushioning revolution – Nike Shox. The highly resilient foam in Nike Shox columns is made of energy efficient material that enhances durability and spring.

Beyond shoes, Nike's range of apparel unifies innovative designs and high-performance fabrics. For example, its FIT technologies manage temperature and moisture to help athletes train and compete in all weather conditions. With Nike's equipment, watches,

PGA ®

Background

The Professional Golfers' Association (PGA) was founded in 1901 and since then it has developed significantly over the last century to become a global brand that is synonymous with golf.

All aspects of the PGA's services are administered from its headquarters at The De Vere Belfry which includes the training and further education of 6,700 members and trainees; membership services and the organisation of tournaments at national and international level. This includes the Ryder Cup where the PGA as Founding Partner works closely with The European Tour as the Managing Partner for the event.

There are seven regional offices located throughout Great Britain and Ireland which have full time staff available to administer the affairs of the Association and support the PGA member. The regional offices also organise tournaments and events for PGA members in the Region and many of these tournaments are connected to charitable causes.

As the oldest PGA in the world, the Association is very conscious of its position as a leader and delivers a reputation that other brands continue to strive for, in terms of its integrity, professionalism, heritage and lifestyle that is widely recognised around the globe.

In the wake of a new breed of golf superstars, the spotlight in sports marketing has therefore turned its attentions to this Royal and Ancient game. Whilst the sport has long enjoyed global success, its re-emergence on mainland Europe and the UK is attracting a host of newcomers to the marketing fairways.

The PGA boasts a Coat of Arms which was introduced in 2001 to celebrate its Centenary and recognise the achievement of a milestone in the development of the professional game.

Achievements

The PGA has been quick to identify the marketing potential it brings to commercial partners via its network of club professionals. Diversity is the key to its success and having the flexibility to tailor initiatives to meet partners' commercial needs.

It therefore adopts an innovative and pioneering focus through its leading influence in developing the growth of the game from grassroots to the grey market.

Proof that the formula is working is highlighted by the recent arrival of a host of new household names that have welcomed the benefit of the PGA umbrella. These include BMW, Bryant Homes, Glenbrae,

> A key influencer in the world of golf spanning 55 countries worldwide

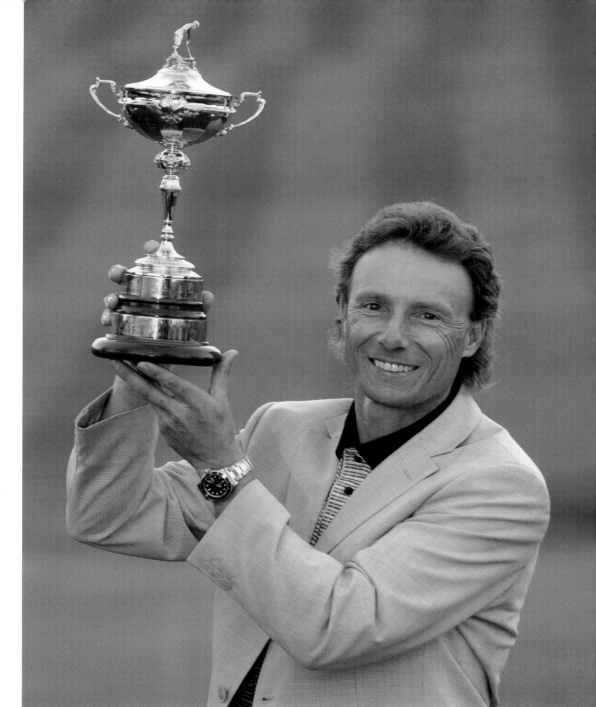

Gulf Air, Jaguar Cars, Nestlé Rowntree, Parker Pens and Red Bull which have joined loyal supporters including Glenmuir, Lombard, Peugeot, The Royal Bank of Scotland and Sunderland generating millions of pounds of investment into the game.

The growing interest in corporate golf is another expanding area for the PGA, which is complementing its partner programmes. Increased demand in this area is being fuelled by the PGA's expertise with its ability to create a professional tournament environment but within a relaxed and friendly atmosphere.

Product/Promotion

Until recently golf has been perceived as a traditional sport aimed predominately at the male fraternity, but that's now all changing. The increasing number of women taking up the game and the introduction of equal opportunities at many golf clubs are providing a catalyst to this significant change.

Brand marketing is therefore exploring new avenues and opportunities as the creative marketers look to lifestyle trends and habits as parallel hooks for their target audience.

The combination of all these factors means that golf has become a major common denominator for companies to associate themselves with, and their brands.

PGA is exploring new opportunities for sponsors including partnerships, product endorsement, merchandising, direct marketing to golfers as well as corporate promotional activity, sponsorship, training and education platforms.

The PGA's website, www.pga.info, provides an essential marketing platform and it regularly receives over a million hits a month with over 150,000 unique users.

Offline, 'PGA Profile' is the members' magazine, published eleven times a year. It provides an excellent medium to promote initiatives to PGA members and carries considerable influence amongst the golf trade market. Meanwhile, PGA Golf Pages is a regional consumer publication produced twice a year.

The PGA Official Yearbook, published annually is distributed to PGA members, the golf trade and to the golfing consumer through independent newsstand distribution.

www.pga.info

prince®

Background

It was in 1970 that Bob McClure, working in his garage, invented Little Prince, the first tennis ball machine for home court use. This signalled the birth of Prince Manufacturing, named after the town of Princeton in the US.

Over the next few years, Howard Head was introduced to the Prince Ball Machine. Frustrated with his tennis game, Howard soon felt compelled to work out a few design bugs in the Ball Machine... and, incredibly, not long afterwards became majority owner and Chairman of the Board.

While the Ball Machine prospered, Head continued to struggle with off-centre hits and lack of control, which motivated him to invent the first patented Prince oversized racquet, the Prince Classic. At 110 square inches, its revolutionary design

PAT RAFTER; PHOTO, GETTY IMAGES

changed the shape of the game and introduced the world to the concept of a 'sweetspot'. The Classic became the most successful racquet of its time.

In 1977, the Prince Graphite established the brand as the material technology leader. The first graphite racquet, adopted by many top players, quickly became the standard by which all others were compared.

The advent of the larger racquet headsize put greater demands on string – so Prince developed its first multi-filament string. The Prince Synthetic Gut continues to maintain its status as the world's best-selling string.

Prince's pioneering R&D expertise produced the Prince Pro, the world's lightest aluminium racquet with which Pat Cash won the Wimbledon title.

In 1982, Prince introduced one of the first Stringing Machines, the P-200, in response to the more practical aspects of the game – and two years later unveiled its first line of tennis wear, continuing its commitment to serve a tennis player's every need. Shortly thereafter, the brand saw the need to go beyond the all-purpose tennis shoe and developed a lightweight and durable shoe for the sport, the TPU-4000.

The brand purchased Ektelon, the global leader in racquetball, in 1987 – and also branched into the international squash market. Within two years of entering the market, Prince

changed the future of squash with the graphite Prince Extender – its longer main strings dramatically enlarging the power zone.

In 1999 Prince introduced the Triple Threat Racquet Series, which offered a revolutionary new weighting system, this technology was the game's first and only racquet technology to offer perfect balance and stability.

Achievements

Prince has revolutionised racquet sports since its conception back in the early 1970s. It has made the game of tennis easier to play with its introductions of the 'Oversize' racquets; it reshaped squash with its innovative 'Extender' racquets; and redefined badminton with its 'Y-Joint' concept. Today, Prince provides game-enhancing equipment for players from head to toe, with shoes, apparel, accessories, and more.

Prince has also been at the heart of some historic wins. Michael Chang won the French Open with the Prince Original Graphite racquet – and seven years later revitalised his career with the Prince Precision Michael Chang LongBody racquet, with which he climbed back up to the number two player in the ATP world rankings. In addition,

A cutting-edge, industry leading sports brand in the development of performance racquet sports equipment

Jennifer Capriati won both the Australian Open and French Open using the Prince Triple Threat Rebel racquet.

In 2000 Prince introduced the MORE Performance line of tennis racquets – the first racquets in history built using a revolutionary PowerLock technology, featuring a unique patented moulding technique that creates string channels so that absolutely no drilling of the racquet is required. It is this technology that was the feature of the MORE Attack racquet which helped Maria Sharapova lift the Wimbledon singles title in such stunning style in 2004 – and led to England's Peter Nicol, celebrating his 60th month as the world's number one squash player in the same year.

Product/Promotion

Prince has enhanced its international exposure by sponsoring some of the most elite athletes in racquet sports,

PETER NICOL: PHOTO, STEPHEN LINE

including tennis legends Stan Smith, Patrick Rafter, Martina Navratilova and more recently Jennifer Capriati, Juan Carlos Ferrero, Guillermo Coria and the Russian teenage sensation and Wimbledon Champion Maria Sharapova; and squash's world number ones Peter Nicol, John White and Cassie Jackman. Their success in Grand Slam competitions has heightened consumer interest in the Prince brand as well as the sport of tennis. Prince continues to maintain a strong presence on the professional circuits through sponsorships and events, working closely with national and local programmes all over the world and developing grassroots opportunities for the next generation of stars in racquet sports.

A new era was unveiled in May 2003 when a new company, Prince Sports, Inc., acquired the rights to the brand from the Benetton Group, its owners since 1990. Led by George Napier, Prince Sports relocated from Italy to Bordentown, New Jersey, the company's birthplace – thereby reinstating its status as the only leading racquet sports company that is American-owned and American-based.

The brand is currently undergoing a major re-launch around the globe, as the new management undertake their commitment to run a focused, co-ordinated and innovative company. Unlike its competitors, Prince is exclusively focused in racquet sports and will maintain and enhance its reputation as a product-driven innovator, producing products which help players play to the best of their ability and 'Rule the Court'.

MARIA SHARAPOVA: PHOTO, GETTY IMAGES

www.princesports.com

Reebok

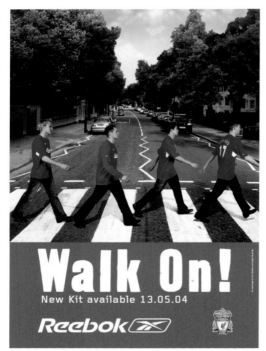

Walk On!
New Kit available 13.05.04

Reebok

Fusing sports performance
with lifestyle and culture

Background

The brand that was to become Reebok initially sprung into life in the UK in the early 1890s when Joseph Williams Foster became the first man to enhance running shoes by fitting them with spikes. Foster quickly developed an international clientele of athletes and by 1958 two of the founder's grandsons had started a companion company that bore the Reebok brand. What followed were a series of distribution agreements that saw Reebok evolve into an international brand. In 1979, such a deal was struck in North America with the introduction of three running shoes for that market, the retail price was US$60 a pair, making them the most expensive such product available. Much of the company's growth has come from its ability to stay in touch with the rapid evolution in the demand for sportswear. The obsession with running in the 1970s was replaced in turn by fitness in the 1980s, football (1990s), music and sports culture (2000). At each step of the way, Reebok planned, initiated and succeeded in launching product lines that catered to the latest trend, firmly establishing itself as one of the most recognisable sports brands in the world.

Achievements

Reebok has long prided itself on keeping track with the latest market movements and many of its achievements to date have stemmed from its ability to gain first mover advantage in various niches of the sportswear sector. In the 1980s, Reebok was the first brand to recognise women's sport and lead the development of aerobics – a category that it still maintains leadership in today. Continuing this trend of innovation, many of Reebok's new product

Reebok
OUTPERFORM

AWARD WINNING ATHLETES WEAR
AWARD WINNING FOOTWEAR

RUNNER'S **EC** EDITORS' CHOICE   Premier Road

RUNNER'S **EC** EDITORS' CHOICE   Premier Road Lite

RUNNER'S **BU** BEST UPDATE   Premier Road Plus

RBK.COM/UK

lines, developed in association with leading athletes of various sports, have become award-winning offerings. Perhaps the most noticeable recent achievement has been the creation of RBK. RBK was born from Reebok's recognition of the growth of two important trends in its consumer base — sports lifestyle and the youth market. Influenced by the styles associated with music and sport, RBK tapped into the culture of its target market and has become a phenomenal success for Reebok. It is not only on the product side that Reebok has made significant strides. In the face of increasing criticism for the sportswear sector concerning the abuse of human rights, the company's decision to launch the Reebok Human Rights Foundation reflected that Reebok was dedicated to combating such issues.

Product/Promotion

Reebok's core target market can be separated into two sectors — sports and youth culture. As could be expected from a global sports brand, much of Reebok's promotional work for the former category runs through its array of endorsement and sponsorship deals with a host of athletes and properties in numerous sports. The brand's strong history of sports marketing across the world, encompasses the likes of Liverpool FC and Bolton Wanderers (football); Andy Roddick (tennis); and Kelly Holmes (athletics). Impressively, Reebok is one of the few brands that can justifiably claim to have cornered US sport. In December 2000, the company signed an exclusive ten-year partnership with the NFL for all of the league's 32 teams. The following year a similar arrangement was agreed with the NBA. Reebok's major global and local advertising campaigns have been at the forefront of such creative work — the award-winning TV ad 'Belly's coming to Get You' being one such recent example. Beyond the core sports market, the creation of the RBK brand moved Reebok beyond its traditional confines into youth culture, music and lifestyle promotions. In 2004, the brand broke new ground with RBK advertising and point of sale campaigns featuring rappers Jay Z and 50 Cent. RBK is also the first brand to launch an endorsed music shoe and sell it commercially, signifying how the brand is interwoven with modern culture.

www.reebok.com

RUSSELL ATHLETIC™

Background

It all started in 1902. In the rural Alexander City, Alabama, a 26 year old man equipped with only ten sewing machines and eight knitting machines set out to realise his dream: starting his own clothing company. That man was Benjamin Russell and he called his brainchild The Russell Manufacturing Company.

The very first products the small factory produced were undershirts for ladies. Despite the lack of electricity, which was not installed until 1912, more then 150 of these were churned out daily.

It wasn't until the beginning of the 1920s that people started to use t-shirts in leisure sports activities. This was the opportunity for Russell Athletic to broaden its horizons.

In 1930 the fleece-lined sweatshirt was introduced, which was quite similar to the ones we know today. Garments like this quickly sparked the interest of several sports teams and they started to commission Russell Athletic to design their uniforms. When in 1932 the Southern Manufacturing Company was acquired, Russell dived

head first into his new role – the design and fabrication of team clothing.

Achievements

In 1967 Russell Athletic reached another milestone with the introduction of the tear away football shirt. The whole idea that clothing could enhance sporting activities was nothing less than revolutionary.

Always quick off the mark, the Russell Company immediately installed an internal research and development team to continue the search for special cuts and fits that addressed the needs of top athletes.

In the early 1990s Russell Athletic scored another homerun when they became the sole and official supplier of game jerseys for Major League Baseball uniforms. Legendary US teams like The Atlanta Braves, The New York Mets, The Boston Red Sox, The San Francisco Giants and The Los Angeles Lakers are now all being equipped with Russell Athletic garments.

The brand's position today is the direct result of one man's vision, talent and hard work: Benjamin Russell. From day one, Russell Athletic has built its name around words like Quality, Durability and Comfort. Today, each one of these words is woven into each and every garment that leaves its factory – every day of every year.

> A distinctive sportswear brand with more than 100 years of experience in outfitting generations of athletes

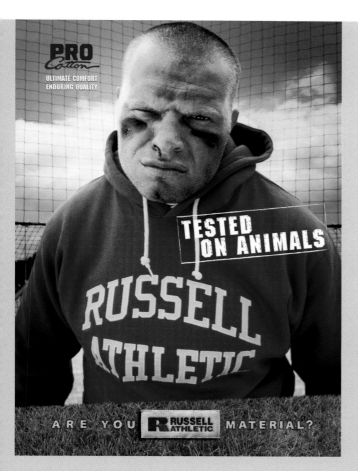

Product/Promotion

Nowadays t-shirts and sweatshirts are part of practically every wardrobe. An important reason for this popularity is the fact that they are honest functional and simple products. No other product offers so much variety in fits, shapes, shades, etc.

There is, however, more to t-shirts and sweatshirts than meets the eye, as the production process is very complex. The process is dependant on specific details such as the construction and dye of the fabric, the specifications of a particular fit, the kind of stitching which is chosen, the use of fabric mixes, the construction of seams and the way arms are cut, as well as the inserts on sides and armholes – the list continues.

It is only through knowledge and attention to detail that the full richness of t-shirts and sweatshirts can come alive. Russell Athletic believes that only if you love and know the product, are you able to bring out its best features. It is due to this dedication that the brand takes pride in what it does. Russell Athletic feels that it is its obligation to deliver the best possible t-shirt and sweatshirt and to exceed expectations.

So no matter whether you are small or tall, or what your individual likes and needs may be, the brand aims to provide garments to suit a full range of requirements.

In 2002 Russell Athletic celebrated its first centennial and what better occasion to bring back some of the legendary detailing that, through the decades, has made Russell Athletic the great brand it is today? Its engineering roots, combined with today's technology for enhanced movement, makes Russell Athletic the fusion of form, function and desire. It is the brand's goal to create the ultimate range of t-shirts and sweatshirts – a range that Russell Athletic hopes will help everyone live active lives better in the 21st century.

It is therefore little surprise that the brand's global mission is:

To be the brand of authentic, athletically inspired, apparel that people can rely on to help them enjoy their healthy lives for the long run. Are You Russell Athletic Material?

SCIENCE IN SPORT

leaders in sports nutrition

Background

In a sporting environment where a fraction of a second can stand between success and failure, servicing the nutritional needs of the top athletes has become a crucial part of preparing for the top events.

Science in Sport (SiS) grew out of the desire to provide the best nutritional products and advice to athletes; be they the biggest names on the world stage, or the keen amateur.

Using the latest in laboratory discoveries, and feedback from the athletes themselves, the brand mixes qualified sport scientists, food technologists, and a physician to develop an unprecedented knowledge bank of the nutritional needs of athletes and produce a range of drug-free products.

SiS was the brainchild of keen sportsman Tim Lawson. An expert in the benefits of highly sophisticated nutrition programmes, he toured the country extolling the virtues to sportsmen and women.

Soon it became apparent there was a demand for better

nutritional products and services, and in 1992 Lawson formed SiS to reconcile feedback with the scientific information available to design, develop and manufacture these products.

Today, its main brands include GO, a hypotonic energy drink; PSP22, a high energy drink; GO Bar, a nutritious energy bar; REGO, a recovery drink; plus the Protein Kinetics System and a range of other supplements. All of which have positioned the brand as leaders in sports nutrition.

Achievements

Initially, SiS grew its reputation by the use of its products in top-level cycling thanks in part to the use and endorsement of its range by Olympic gold medallist Chris Boardman, who liked the company ethos, and helped to inspire the creation of REGO, total recovery sports fuel.

It wasn't long before the word began to spread and SiS's products became more popular at the top level of many other sports. To date its products

Continually striving to innovate and improve products to assist all athletes to reach their goals

have helped athletes to win Olympic golds, world championships, Premiership soccer titles and set numerous world records.

The brand prides itself on designing, developing and manufacturing its own products to ensure they are of the highest standard; frequently working in tandem with the top universities to be the first with the major breakthroughs, drug-free and without any unnecessary additives.

One such achievement was when it developed the world's first isotonic energy gel, GO Gel, and the first textured energy bar, GO Bar, with no added sugar and less than 2% fat. It also pioneered the Protein Kinetics concept as applied to recovery and adaptation to exercise.

The brand's products regularly top sports magazines' product tests for performance and taste, among its many successes being named Nutritional Product of the Year by Runners' World.

Product/Promotion

SiS has built its brand through a strategy of associating with the best of today's sports men and women.

Its most recent marketing campaign focused on isotonic energy gel GO Gel, where lacking the clout of a global company proved little problem to extolling the brand's virtues.

SiS drew on the testimonies and real life experiences of world class athletes to back up its statement of leaders in sports nutrition. An advertising, PR and promotional activity programme was channelled directly into sports specific media sponsorship of events and attending sports exhibitions. Because of the proven success of the products and the trust developed between the brand and top athletes, SiS has generated a deep level of brand loyalty. Cyclist Bradley Wiggins, for example, has used SiS products from first attending a SiS nutrition seminar when he was just thirteen years old to winning three medals at the Athens Olympics. Olympic bronze medallist swimmer Stephen Parry took part in early product research as an age group swimmer and has stayed with the SiS brand since.

Other well known names it has deals in place with include MotoGP rider Neil Hodgson, triple jump star Ashia Hansen and explorer Sir Ranulph Fiennes.

Now SiS is the trusted choice of sports champions from Premier League football through motor racing to extreme sports. Its brands have been to the top of Everest and travelled from Pole to Pole; across the deserts and oceans of the world.

SCOTTISH
RUGBY

Background

From the beginnings of the sport in Scotland to its recently unveiled new branding strategy, the Scottish Rugby Union (SRU) has played a pivotal role in the development and administration of the game.

As the governing body for rugby union north of the border, the brand's primary purpose is to support and promote the sport from grassroots to the most senior international level.

From funding community development schemes, to running coaching courses; from regulating competitions to registering players; the SRU's role is far more than just marketing and financing the sport.

Its most high-profile asset is that of the Scotland national team. The SRU estimates that around 75% of the income it generates comes through the international arena.

The national team is based at Murrayfield Stadium, which has a capacity of 67,500 in Edinburgh, which has been the home of Scottish rugby since 1925. A single, full house international match at Murrayfield (between Scotland and a visiting national team) can generate as much as £5 million for the SRU through ticket receipts and TV revenue, £10 million for the economy in Edinburgh and around £20 million for the wider Scottish economy.

In addition to the Six Nations Championship, in which it battles England, Ireland, Wales, France and Italy, Scotland also hosts an autumn series against some of the big southern hemisphere teams such as Australia, South Africa and New Zealand. Additional summer matches are also played with regular tours overseas.

The SRU also presides over the domestic game. The majority of the Scotland squad play for one of the nation's three professional clubs — Edinburgh Rugby, Glasgow Rugby and The Borders. Below the three pro-teams are around 240 amateur clubs who play in national and district league and cup competitions.

Brand extensions include Scottish Rugby Events — offering supporter travel packages; Scottish Rugby Direct — an online retail business targeting the ex-pat market; and Murrayfield Tours — giving fans a sneak peak behind the scenes of the famous venue.

Achievements

Regardless of on pitch performance the brand continues to grow year on year. Inevitably, a good run by the national team will see gate receipts rocket, merchandise sales soar and media interest swell.

2003 saw Scotland reach the quarter-final of the Rugby World Cup in Australia, beating off Japan and the USA, as well as Fiji en-route, thus reaching the last eight and guaranteeing qualification to the finals in 2007.

In 2002, South Africa were humbled at Murrayfield — the first time Scotland had beaten the tourists since 1969. In 2000, a 19-13 home win against England won the Calcutta Cup — a trophy the two teams have competed for each time they have met in international competition since 1879.

And in 1999, wins over Wales, Ireland and France were enough to clinch the final Five Nations Championship, before Italy was added to the tournament's ranks.

While silverware has not come easily in recent years, the emphasis going into the future, according to a major strategic review carried out in 2004, is very much on improving the overall team performance at all

New Vision, New Leadership, New Winning Culture

www.scottishrugby.org

international levels, and to making the necessary investment in the major clubs to ensure Scotland is represented in the latter stages of the top club competitions. Scottish Rugby's growth in interest and participation is faster than any other sport in Scotland.

Product/Promotion

A recent major overhaul of the image and strategy of the SRU has resulted in a new identity being born, encapsulating the key brand values of dynamism, power and passion.

A striking new logo featuring a 3D rugby ball emblazoned with the traditional Scottish thistle, is fronting a new approach to help identify and market Scottish rugby.

The brand power that lies within the national team and its personalities will play a key role in a new push to build the appeal of the Scotland brand, while creating awareness of the key focus of the brand strategy.

An extensive PR strategy will work alongside a cross-platform advertising campaign, email and online initiative and direct mail scheme to communicate with fans both new and old. Other programmes aimed at extending the brand and introducing new tools will also play a vital role.

SHIMANO®

Background

Shimano has made an art form out of the manufacture of sporting technological material, particularly in terms of bicycle components and fishing equipment. The brand was born in 1921 in Japan when Shozaburo Shimano established the Shimano Iron Works and began production of the bicycle freewheel.

Pursuit of dreams through the enjoyment of nature

Within ten years, Shimano had made a huge success of honing his craft and began to export his product line to the four corners of the globe. Following the development of cold forging technologies in the early 1960s, the Shimano business had grown to the extent of being able to begin fully-fledged sales in the lucrative US market with entry into the European market following shortly after in 1965. Five years later and the Shimano product range diversified when a specialist fishing tackle division was launched. Such was the success of the product development initiative that

offshore production plants began to crop up in key markets and the company registered a stock listing on the Osaka Securities Exchange. New product ranges continued to place Shimano at the forefront of its market and by 1988, coinciding with the establishment of its UK operation, the brand had expanded its output even further with the introduction of cycling footwear. The following two decades continued this trend of market building with an action sports division set up in 1997. All through its history, Shimano has accompanied product innovation with the introduction of new regional operations, an evolution that has turned it into a truly global brand.

Achievements

Whether it be the competitive edge on a racing bike or the latest engineering in fishing rods, Shimano components have led the way in terms of technological and design advancements. The brand's work on developing high performance bicycle components has taken it into new areas of achievement. The recent introduction of innovative high performance wheels reduces weight and aerodynamic drag without sacrificing strength. The Shimano Automatic Inter-3

Mountain Bike Race, nationally known multi-day events attended by thousands of bicycle racers and cycling enthusiasts. All of the marketing activity is underpinned by Shimano's business philosophy of developing products that help people to interact with nature through the outdoor activities they love.

www.shimano.com

and Inter-8 systems have also enabled the provision of completely automatic shifting using a CPU-controlled internally geared hub. It allows the cyclist to enjoy multi-speed cycling without worrying about how or when to shift gears. Another product innovation has been Flight Deck – an advanced, component-integrated cycling computer that provides an extensive array of information – while Dura-Ace road-racing components are the result of the 'stress-free' design philosophy that Shimano has been a market leader in. Similar product achievements have been made in enhancing the fishing experience. The polished high-tech appearance of the product range is appealing to the eye while offering precision operation to the hand. The advanced technology created by Shimano has been applied on a human scale to enhance human performance.

Product/Promotion

As way of a marketing strategy, Shimano is committed to actively promoting the sports in which its products are used. The company has an ever-growing sponsorship portfolio and schedule of activities that support and encourage cycling and sport fishing around the world. The brand sponsors numerous tournaments, and holds fishing seminars, often attended by well-known outdoorsmen, designed to introduce anglers to the latest techniques used in sport fishing.

Shimano also provides neutral technical support at all major cycling events like the World Cycling Championships and the World Cup for mountain bikes. The company actively sponsors and provides technical support not only to well-known professional cycling teams such as Lampre of Italy and the US Postal Service Team, but also to amateur teams regardless of the type of equipment they ride.

In addition, Shimano is supported by the likes of Lance Armstrong, six time winner of the Tour de France, who rides using Shimano equipment.

In Japan, Shimano is the driving force behind the Shimano Suzuka Road Race and the Shimano

speedo

Background

Speedo is one of the most recognisable brand names in the world. Founded in 1910 by Scotsman Alexander MacRae following his emigration to Australia, the company originally began life as a hosiery manufacturer before turning its attention to swimwear in 1914. The Speedo brand came into being in 1928 coinciding with more liberal attitudes towards bathing and the growth of swimming as a sport. The name itself was the result of a staff competition to brand a new swimming costume. When an employee by the name of Captain Parsonson coined the slogan 'Speed on in your Speedos' a franchise was born. Prior to the launch of the first

Speedo branded costume, all swimwear had been made from wool. From such beginnings, the Speedo brand soon became synonymous with market-leading performance swimwear, branching out beyond its Australian roots into the global market. Speedo began manufacturing in the UK in the 1970s when it became the first company to produce nylon/Lycra swimwear which remains the most popular fabric today. The company also began producing beach and leisurewear, extending the Speedo brand beyond competition swimsuits. In 1991, Speedo was acquired by the London-based Pentland Group — owner of a number of other sports, outdoor and fashion brands. The change in

ownership did not deter Speedo from its path of innovation and the brand continues to launch new market-leading product ranges, underpinned by the latest technologies and design, as it has done throughout its history.

Achievements

Over its 75 years of performance swimwear manufacture Speedo has been at the forefront of swimwear technology. The quality of its products is illustrated through a list of the achievements of the swimmers who swear by the brand. From the 1956 Melbourne Olympics, where the Australian team kitted out in Speedo swimwear swept the board with eight gold medals, through to the 1992 Barcelona Games where over half of the medals were won by swimmers wearing Speedo, the brand has consistently excelled. It was at the latter Olympics that Speedo launched the world's first 'fast swimwear' fabric, the S2000. This culture of innovation also spawned the revolutionary full-body performance swimsuit Fastskin, unveiled in 2000, which further improves flexibility and performance. At the Sydney Games that year, 83% of all medals won were by athletes wearing Speedo. The Fastskin concept was further developed for the 2004 Athens Games to create Fastskin FSII,

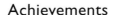

Revolutionary, record-breaking swimwear

FASTSKIN FSII

A NEW BREED HAS EVOLVED

FASTSKIN FSII™: AN AQUALAB™ PRODUCTION FROM SPEEDO®. FEATURING UP TO 4% LESS DRAG THAN WORLD RECORD-BREAKING FASTSKIN®.
SPECIAL EFFECTS: DUAL FASTSKIN AND FLEXSKIN FABRICS, TURBULENCE MANAGEMENT SYSTEM AND NEUTRALISER. ENGINEERED TO MIMIC SHARK DYNAMICS, REDUCE DRAG AND OPTIMISE
PERFORMANCE. AVAILABLE IN GENDER AND STROKE-SPECIFIC SUITS. STARRING: JENNY THOMPSON (USA)   KOSUKE KITAJIMA (JPN)   KATY SEXTON (GBR)   MICHAEL KLIM (AUS)
INGE DE BRUIJN (NED)   MICHAEL PHELPS (USA)   GRANT HACKETT (AUS)   HANNAH STOCKBAUER (GER)   LENNY KRAYZELBURG (USA)   AMANDA BEARD (USA)   MASSIMILIANO ROSOLINO (ITA)
FASTSKIN FSII™: A SWIMWEAR EVOLUTION CREATING A SWIMMING REVOLUTION. APPEARING SOON AT A POOL NEAR YOU.

now showing at **www.speedoaqualab.com**   aqualab

using ground-breaking technology based on analysis of the drag and flow of water around swimmers. At Athens, five out of the eight world records were broken by swimmers donning the Speedo brand.

Product/Promotion

While best known as the world's leading swimwear brand, Speedo has also grown, in recent years, into the wider fashion market with its leisurewear product range where it is in the process of establishing itself in the wider fashion swimwear, accessories and beach apparel market.

Speedo invests in a full range of communication channels to support this growing product range. Unsurprisingly for a brand so closely allied with swimming, Speedo has a number of endorsees, including world leading swimmers such as Australia's Grant Hackett and US phenomenon Michael Phelps who was the first swimmer in the history of the Olympics to win eight medals at one Games – of course wearing the new Fastskin FSII. This is supported by advertising and communications initiatives. For example, at the Sydney 2000 Olympics, Speedo ran a number of promotions conveying the brand message that 'winners wear Speedo' – a campaign that featured prominently a number of the brand's sponsored swimmers. The activity is not limited to major sporting events. To celebrate its 75th anniversary

in 2003, Speedo introduced a retro-style logo to accompany its advertising and point-of-sale material with its anniversary celebrations promoted through a range of PR and marketing campaigns. Looking forward, advertising will play a central role in growing Speedo's share of the beach leisurewear market as it aims to reposition itself as a desirable and fashionable brand with a consistent and appealing image. In line with its desire to expand into new markets, Speedo has also extended its stable of elite athletes to include Louise Moore and

Dan Nott, the 2004 UK National Wakeboarding champions beginning a new chapter in the Speedo story.

www.speedo.com

TaylorMade®

Background

TaylorMade-adidas Golf sits high on the leader-board of global sport brands.

Founded in 1979, it has become synonymous with the game of golf and is today also responsible for developing and marketing apparel and footwear for adidas Golf, as well as balls and accessories for the Maxfli brand.

It's all a long way from its first emergence on the scene when founder Gary Adams brought to life the first ever 'Metal-wood' golf club, which has been the core product line for the brand ever since.

A sales representative for the PGA Golf brand, Adams had been approached by someone in 1978 wanting to find investors to buy into the metal-headed driver they were developing. Adams was interested and a year later, after numerous modifications, Adams' newly-formed TaylorMade brand – a name chosen to indicate the

clubs were 'tailored' for better players – introduced its creation and was met with huge demand.

The brand's impact on the golf industry saw it quickly grow and establish itself as one of the major players; a position further enhanced when, in 1984, it became part of the Salomon group.

In 1997, when Salomon and adidas teamed up, it joined with adidas Golf to become a wholly-owned subsidiary of adidas-Salomon AG.

With adidas now able to access the increasingly lucrative golf marketplace, and TaylorMade able to tap into the vast resources being part of the group presented, it has continued to grow, and now boasts a portfolio which includes drivers, fairway woods, utility clubs, irons, wedges, putters, plus a range of bags, headwear and other accessories.

Achievements

Ever since Gary Adams first marketed the metal-headed Pittsburgh Persimmon 25 years ago, TaylorMade has always endeavoured to continue introducing the innovation and design advancements needed to remain at the cutting edge of the industry.

It made its first Tour appearance in the 1979 Tournament of

The TaylorMade brand is about being authentic, passionate, innovative and competitive in the world of golf

Champions, a move which helped establish its position as the club of choice for professionals and serious amateurs.

By the early 1980s, courtesy of utilising the marketing tagline 'the clubs the pros play', TaylorMade's sales soared, and its expansion saw it develop a research and development centre in Carlsbad, California. The brand would eventually move its headquarters there too following Salomon's takeover of the firm in 1984.

Sales quickly rocketed to more than £80 million and by the start of the 1990s, the brand had a 34% market share. Such was its success in the US, it pushed out globally, and set up subsidiaries in the UK, France and Japan.

TaylorMade continued to keep pushing back the boundaries, with products such as the Raylor fairway wood, one of the first utility clubs, and the innovative and complex Bubble Shaft.

In 2004, TaylorMade again broke through the technology barrier with the r7 quad and r5 Dual drivers, featuring moveable and fixed-weight technology. Since its launch in June 2004, the r7 quad driver has experienced unprecedented success on Tour and in the market place prompting one respected golf journalist to call it 'the equipment launch of the decade'.

To underline its success, the brand is currently the number one driver used by players on the professional circuits worldwide, in addition to the top selling metal-wood globally (Source: Darrell Survey/Sports Marketing Surveys).

Product/Promotion

Sponsoring the biggest names on the circuit has always been the backbone of TaylorMade's marketing efforts.

Each player serves as a brand ambassador, with the likes of Sergio Garcia, Retief Goosen, Mike Weir and Darren Clarke not only generating coverage during televised events, but also utilised in a broad spectrum of marketing materials from advertising to in-store, point-of-sale materials.

In 2004, TaylorMade rolled out a new brand concept; 'What drives you?' It features as a brand sign-off in all its above-the-line marketing creative, and will be an integral part of all marketing and brand activity during 2005.

Retail marketing, advertising and PR are key parts of the communications mix — all of which were heavily utilised for the significant campaign to promote the launch of the r7 quad driver; a launch supported by the biggest media and PR campaign in the brand's history.

The cross media assault underlined once again TaylorMade's golfing credentials — and sends a very clear signal to its competitors that it is seeking only to further reinforce its position at the top.

www.taylormadegolf.com

Background

Triumph is a family run company and was founded in Germany in 1886. The brand's early ranges included Triumph Sportswear, Triumph Sport and Golden Cup.

The brand has become one of the leading underwear producers in the world and in 2003 had an annual turnover of 1.6 billion Euros, and 38,691 employees. Famous for having 'the bra for the way you are', Triumph was one of the first companies to recognise that a bra worn for sport should meet special criteria – its first sports bra was launched around 30 years ago. Since then, the designs have been continuously updated, improved and adapted as technology and fabrics have advanced.

The sub-brand Triumph Tri-Action was registered by Triumph some time before it was actually used and the brand's first sports bras were not sold under this name. As the name 'Tri-Action' suggests, all bras give three essential kinds of support: from above, with ergonomically shaped, stretch non-slip straps; from the sides, with full coverage cups; and from below, with broad underbust bands to prevent slipping.

As an innovative and highly functional sports range made by Triumph, all products achieve the individual requirements women have while exercising. Triumph Tri-Action stands for first class function, freedom of movement, maximum support and maximum comfort.

Triumph products are now distributed throughout Europe in specialist lingerie shops, department stores, mail order and other home shopping channels as well as through sports retailers and sports associations.

Achievements

Since 1980 the female German Olympic team has worn Triumph sports bras. Other European countries also supply their teams on an occasional basis. In the UK, the British Olympic Ladies team were 'supported' by Triumph for the 1996 Olympics in Atlanta. Over 200 ladies were individually measured and advised on the most suitable Triumph bra for them.

The Triumph Tri-Action Workout bra is regularly recognised for its effectiveness in 'Tried & Tested' features in the press.

Product/Promotion

Quality is at the heart of the Triumph brand and all products are designed to meet the needs of women. The sports bras are therefore always made from high performance fabrics that regulate body temperature, offer comfort and absorb moisture. This technology allows perspiration to be taken away from the skin to the outer surface of the bra where it evaporates. Cotton used to be an important part of the fabric composition, but sophisticated microfibres with special features, such as odour inhibitors, are now increasingly used.

All Triumph Tri-Action bras are comfortable, supportive and won't slip or chafe. Special features include seamfree cups, cushioning, extra flat seaming and binding as well as specially positioned fasteners to eliminate irritation.

Sports bras 'for the way you are'

advice as well as a website, www.triumph-international.co.uk, where the range is showcased.

To increase awareness of the brand, on-going PR work targets health, beauty, fashion and features press on newspapers, consumer magazines and specialist publications, as well as TV and radio on the importance of the sports bra. Triumph Tri-Action sports bras have featured in Triumph's national advertising campaigns.

Triumph is positioned as the company that understands women and has 'the bra for the way you are'.

www.triumph-international.co.uk

The Tri-Action Powermove also features stretch padded cups with special underwires that expand and realign themselves as you move to give a personalised fit. Meanwhile the Tri-Action Pulsebeat has three tabs on the inside of the underbust band into which a heart rate monitor can be slipped. The bra can, of course, also be worn without this.

A team of countrywide in-store consultants plays an important role in educating consumers about the importance of wearing a sports bra and advising on correct size and suitability of specific bra types. Most women in the UK still do not know their correct bra size, so this is viewed as an extremely important service.

Triumph also has a consumer enquiry line which offers

Background

It is not underestimating the impact of the Twenty20 Cup to say that the competition breathed new life into domestic cricket in the UK. While international cricket is still a major public draw, by the end of the 2002 season it was clear that the domestic professional game needed invigorating. In particular, attendances and viewing figures for the Benson & Hedges Cup, which the Twenty20 Cup replaced, were stalling and domestic cricket was not attracting enough of the younger fans that are the lifeblood of any sport.

The England and Wales Cricket Board (ECB), cricket's national governing body, undertook significant research which

suggested that a shorter, more exciting format was needed to bring a larger, younger and more diverse audience back to domestic cricket. Hence the introduction of the Twenty20 Cup in 2003. This new format – just 20 overs per team – reduced the length of the games significantly, creating a high action two hour 45 minute package. In order to maximise accessibility, all group games were played in mid summer with matches starting at 5.30pm. With additional excitement created at matches through the use of music, including live bands performing on Finals Day, and other off the field entertainment, the ECB effectively switched the focus towards a more all-round live

experience for the spectator. The event closed with both semi-finals and the final played on the same day.

Achievements

The Twenty20 Cup's most notable impact came in its effect on attendance levels for domestic cricket. In year one, more than 230,000 spectators attended the group games of the competition – an astonishing rise of 353% compared to equivalent games in the 2002 Benson & Hedges Cup. With even more viewers tuning in through the ECB's exclusive live rights deal with broadcast network Sky Sports, the competition brought unprecedented levels of interest, and a big rise in attendance, to domestic cricket.

Proving that the initial season was no flash in the pan, a 50-year record crowd of 27,509 gathered for the Middlesex vs Surrey group match at Lord's in 2004. Over 100,000 tickets were sold for matches before the competition began, ensuring attendances rose by 12% in year two, despite the indifferent weather.

The format has caught the attention of the wider cricketing world. South Africa introduced a successful domestic Twenty20

Sparking new life into cricket

Cup competition in 2003 and a number of other cricket nations are set to follow suit. The England Women's team played New Zealand in the first ever Twenty20 international match in 2004 and a number of men's international games are now also scheduled, including an England vs Australia fixture during the 2005 Ashes tour.

Product/Promotion

The responsibility for local promotion and for filling grounds falls to each individual county cricket club. Given the new concept, and the desire to both build brand awareness from existing cricket supporters and attract a new, younger audience to the game, the ECB has done much to build the profile of the competition. It has conducted a major PR and marketing campaign each year, working closely with the competition's sponsors, to boost levels of awareness as it has sought to establish the Twenty20 Cup as an anticipated fixture in each summer's sporting calendar. The focus of all the ECB's initiatives has been to promote the competition to a younger and more family-centric audience highlighting the live entertainment factor that is prevalent at each match both on and off the playing field.

www.ecb.co.uk

TWICKENHAM
THE HOME OF ENGLAND RUGBY

Background

Twickenham's status within English culture is universally renowned for its towering rugby stadium – the stage for England's home international matches. The arena first began hosting England rugby games in 1910 when over 20,000 spectators turned up to watch a game against Wales. From that point onwards, the stadium has

Home of English Rugby

become the official headquarters of English rugby. The origins of Twickenham come from the need of the Rugby Football Union (RFU) to establish a regular home for international games. In the 40 years between the governing body's formation in 1871 and 1910, no fewer than a dozen different grounds had been used for such matches. William Williams, an RFU committee member, was tasked with finding a suitable area and, after much searching he decided upon a ten and a quarter acre

market garden near Twickenham, twelve miles from the centre of London. The land was purchased for £5,572.12s.6d in 1907 and construction work began in 1908. From an initial capacity of 30,000, the stadium has grown over the years to its present intake of up to 74,000 spectators. This process has had its setbacks – the ground was damaged in World War II whilst being used as a Civil Service depot leaving much of the South terrace in disrepair. However the erection of a new South Stand in 1981 followed by subsequent rebuilding work between 1991 and 1995 has brought the ground up to the level it is today.

Achievements

The largest dedicated rugby stadium in the world, Twickenham has played host to a number of high profile clashes, not only between the England international team and their various opponents but also for the end of season climax of the domestic club rugby season.

For all these games, the stadium is invariably full to the rafters. Such is the demand for tickets that the RFU has opted to increase the capacity of the ground still further to 82,000 with the proposed development of the South Stand. Due for completion during 2007, the new South Stand will include a 156 bedroom four star hotel, health & fitness centre, conference and banqueting facilities, dual use performing arts centre, a new Rugby Store and office accommodation for RFU staff.

Product/Promotion

While Twickenham is renowned principally for its rugby heritage, the stadium has evolved into a commercial arena that can stage a variety of events including music concerts and festivals in addition to sporting fixtures. As well as promoting their variety of match day commercial partners around the ground, the RFU

also promotes the stadium on its ability to provide additional functions such as corporate hospitality. The Twickenham Experience Ltd has been set up as a subsidiary company to provide such facilities as well as conference and banqueting offerings. Stadium tours have also proved prosperous with the creation of the Museum of Rugby in 1996 providing an additional focus for such visits. As well as offering a unique insight into the history of the stadium and the sport that it encapsulates, the Museum is also the current home of the Webb Ellis Cup, allocated to rugby's world champions, following England's Rugby World Cup victory in 2003. The stadium tour and Museum of Rugby have also proved a useful promotional tool in the RFU's continuing grass-roots work with schools. Children are regular visitors to Twickenham through organised sessions.

www.rfu.com

teams in the tournament were kitted out in UMBRO, including eventual winners England – a relationship that continues to this day. In 1985, the brand expanded its product range beyond playing kit, introducing the first UMBRO boot in Brazil. The last five years have seen the brand refocus under new ownership, concentrating on reaffirming its mission to inspire and excite the world of football.

Achievements

Celebrating 80 years in football this year, UMBRO's effect on the evolution of playing and training kit and equipment has been significant. Since the turn of the century alone, UMBRO has introduced a revolutionary new Sportswool material, launched the XAI football boot technology and developed the first reversible jersey for an international team. The latest product line to come from the brand is X-Static, used in the new England away kit. The innovative material enhances the body's natural temperature regulation system, keeping the player cool when it's warm and vice versa. Anti-microbial properties in the clothing also reduce the risk of bacteria growth.

Recent years have seen UMBRO branch out into the fashion market to take advantage of the increasing overlap between the global markets for sports clothing and footwear as well as the leisurewear sector. Young UK designer Kim Jones has just completed his third collection for the brand, which mixes fashion while retaining the brand's

Background

Football fans across the world would immediately recognise the double diamond symbol of the UMBRO brand. A logo that was created in 1924 by the Humphrey brothers from their small workshop in Wilmslow, Cheshire has evolved into the face of an international product range sold in over 90 countries.

The growth of the brand has stemmed from its close ties with the football community,

beginning in 1930 when Manchester City won the FA Cup final sporting an UMBRO kit. After a break enforced by the war, during which the company switched to shirt production for the armed forces, UMBRO grew quickly into an internationally renowned brand. The Brazilian national team signed up to wear UMBRO kit during their consecutive World Cup wins in 1958 and 1962. By 1966, fifteen out of the sixteen participating

Inspiring and exciting the world of football

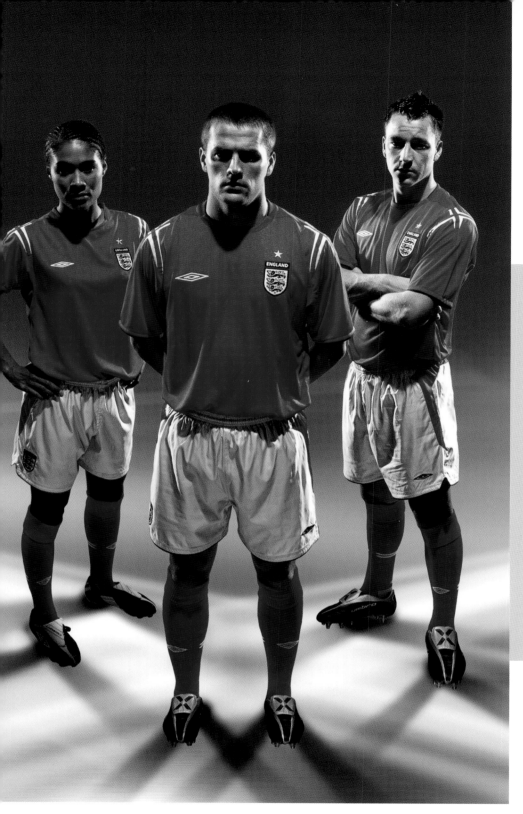

extended the association to run until 2010. Other national team sponsorships include Sweden, Republic of Ireland and Norway. UMBRO also has domestic deals in place with a number of prominent clubs including Chelsea (England), Olympique Lyonnais (France), Celta Vigo (Spain) and FC Santos (Brazil). Sponsorship is not restricted to teams with the recent signing of a fifteen-year deal with England striker Michael Owen, one of the largest such contracts ever announced in football. Owen joins the likes of John Terry, Michel Salgado and Deco in endorsing the UMBRO brand.

Internationally the UMBRO group operates principally through a network of 47 licensees who source and distribute products to sports retail customers. They work closely with the group to maintain a global and uniform UMBRO brand identity. Latterly, emphasis has been placed on the brand's revitalised website as well as viral marketing as its predominant promotional outlets.

influences from terrace culture and football iconology. The range is available across the globe within key fashion boutiques and department stores. UMBRO's advancements have not been restricted to clothing with the launch of the new Digital ball in 2003 winning the rating approval of the sport's governing body FIFA.

Product/Promotion
UMBRO's promotional stance has always been to prove its dedication to every facet of the game, from professional football for both men and women through to beach soccer and futsal. Its close ties with the sport have been outwardly shown predominantly through its sponsorship of over 150 teams worldwide. The most prominent of these is the long-term England kit deal, the latest renewal contract of which

www.umbro.com

ⓌWilson.

Background

Built on a rich heritage of innovation within US sports, the Wilson brand is now globally acknowledged as one of the leading producers of equipment and clothing.

From tennis to golf, baseball to basketball, the Wilson Sporting Goods Company has played a significant role in the development of the sports and today proclaims itself the world's leading tennis brand.

Created in 1913, as a subsidiary of a Chicago meat packing firm, Schwartzchild and Sulzberger, it initially sold by-products of animal gut, such as strings for violins and tennis rackets.

Quickly taken over by a New York banking firm and named after its first chief, Thomas E Wilson, initial success fuelled a growth in its own range of products, among them tennis rackets, baseball gloves and leather balls.

Acquisitions and mergers saw it continue to rise in prominence and develop manufacturing operations across the US.

By the 1940s it expanded into sportswear and established an 'advisory staff' of top athletes to field test and offer recommendations on how best to improve their products, a practice it continues to this day.

Through the 1960s, 1970s – when it was acquired by PepsiCo – and 1980s it continued to expand globally, setting up wholly-owned subsidiary companies through Europe and Asia.

In 1989, Wilson was acquired by its present owner, the fitness equipment firm Amer Sports Group, based in Helsinki, Finland. With the goal of becoming the number one sports equipment company in the world with brands including Atomic, Suunto and Precor, Amer has provided Wilson with the financial support backing required to continue its expansion.

Achievements

Noticeable firsts include production of the first ever valve inflated American football and the first hermetically-sealed tennis ball can.

In the late 1930s, its technicians used controlled hydraulics to bond several layers of wood together to produce Strata-Bloc woods – the biggest innovation in golf since the steel shaft, providing players with more power and direction. It applies a similar technology to its tennis rackets.

And in 1941 it struck a deal which remains to this day one of the most valuable to its brand building endeavours as Wilson's Duke American football became the official ball of the National Football League (NFL).

Focusing on innovation through technology and development for amateur and professional athletes

Wilson **W/S** Staff

Its Jack Kramer Autograph tennis rackets would go on to sell more than ten million units finally being phased out in 1981. Among those using the rackets were the likes of John McEnroe, Arthur Ashe and Chris Evert.

Furthermore, it proved to lead from the front of the production line too, when, in 1949 it became the first company in the sporting goods industry to use a computer for inventory control.

Since then it has evolved as a brand and in its range of products, pioneered the design of baseball gloves, recent improvements in volleyballs and has seen huge

benefits from associations with the biggest names in sport.

Product/Promotion

A core part of Wilson's strategy is conveying its brand values through associations with leading sporting events – a platform from which it showcases its latest ground-breaking equipment.

A recent deal saw it extend its relationship with the International Tennis Federation (ITF) to retain its position as the official ball of its Davis Cup competition and other ITF initiatives until 2007.

Its position in the tennis marketplace is further enhanced

through personal deals with the likes of Serena and Venus Williams and Roger Federer.

In golf, its Wilson Staff brand is to be re-launched with a complete new range of clubs and accessories, designed to 'reassert its premium credentials' it has received a warm response from the golfing fraternity.

As part of the new branding exercise, the Wilson Staff shield, first used in 1960, has been re-modelled and updated to feature across the full range of products, including those used on the Tour by winning Ryder Cup team member Padraig Harrington.

Harrington has also played a key role in developing a number of the new clubs as a member of the elite Wilson Staff Advisory panel.

The re-branding exercise has been conducted with the help of another Chicago-based organisation – VSA Partners Inc – that reshaped the identity and fortunes of Harley-Davidson in recent years.

The new range will be supported by a global advertising and promotional campaign.

www.wilson.com

colours used around the grounds and the lack of commercial logos makes Wimbledon instantly recognisable amongst sporting events.

Hosted in the plush surroundings of The All England Lawn Tennis Club in South West London, it hosted its first annual tournament in 1877 at its original site, before moving to its familiar home in 1922.

Its array of grass courts surrounding its showcase Centre Court, has expanded over the years, and with the new Number One Court Stadium, Millennium Building and Broadcast Centre, the venue has been developed into a modern sports complex providing first class facilities for the 500,000 spectators who now make the annual pilgrimage to what remains globally acknowledged as one of the highlights of the sporting calendar.

Achievements

It is undeniably an achievement in itself that in today's commercially driven sports arena, Wimbledon remains true to its ideals of letting nothing detract from the passion and purity of the sport it showcases.

Blue-chip commercial partners continue to pay the top rate to be associated with the event, and do so through a variety of more sophisticated means, prompting a level of sponsorship exploitation which compliments and feeds off the event's brand values.

Television coverage of the event – it claims to be the world's most widely televised tennis tournament – continues to grow year-on-year with more than 160 territories broadcasting the event.

Not a brand to rest on its laurels, the millions of pounds generated by the annual tournament have been diverted either to grassroots

Background

In today's top-level sports scene, the issue of commercial clutter and how to achieve stand-out in such an environment provides even the most sophisticated marketer sleepless nights.

Yet The Championships, Wimbledon, stands out as a beacon of how to deliver top value to your partners, while keeping the playing arena free from sponsors and advertisers tussling for attention.

Soaked in history, The Championships have become the envy of events around the world, with its clean approach, unique grass surface in today's Grand Slam circuit, and its sophisticated image. The strong use of Wimbledon's official logos, together with its purple and green

Pursuing an aim to continue to be acknowledged as the world's premier tennis tournament

UK and trade press, at regular intervals from October onwards. Advance show court sales are conducted through a public ballot, such is the demand, months before the first bowl of strawberries and cream have been served up.

A handful of tickets sold on the gate each day during the fortnight regularly sees people camping out overnight along the streets lining the venue in a bid to secure them.

Aware of the need to balance out the obvious demand from corporate hospitality partners and that of the regular tennis fan, the All England Club has taken steps to ensure both are happy with their allocation. Under 10% of Centre Court and Number One court tickets are for corporate customers.

The only determining factor in terms of general ground entry during the fortnight is the uncertain nature of the English weather – the one thing even the ever image conscious All England Club cannot control – yet.

initiatives overseen by the Lawn Tennis Association, or to improving the facilities at the ground.

A major strategy to upgrade facilities for spectators, players and media alike has resulted in massive changes in recent years, including a new Number One court which now boasts more than 11,429 seats and improvements to Centre Court, which now houses 13,808.

In the years to come, a retractable roof will be put in place above the Centre Court in a bid to avoid the wash-outs so unavoidable in an English summer, and more seating added, bringing the primary show court up to a 15,000 capacity.

Product/Promotion

With its distinctive green and purple colour scheme and logo, the Wimbledon brand has, unsurprisingly, branched out.

Courtesy of an extensive licensing programme, marketed internationally with help from sports marketing giant IMG, it lends its image to sports, luxury and lifestyle products ranging from computer games to chinaware; chocolate to umbrellas.

Its numerous partners also assist in spreading the brand's image through carefully selected product promotions.

Tickets for the fortnight need little promotion although the event is advertised in the national

www.wimbledon.org

NICK CLARKE

UK Sales Director, Royal Marbella Group
www.royalmarbellagroup.com

For 26 years the Royal Marbella Group has been in the business of making dreams a reality for thousands of people. With a vast land bank in the most desirable locations on the Costa del Sol, Baleric and Canary islands and with 4,000 properties under varying stages of construction, Royal Group specialising in matching clients financial, geographical and lifestyle requirements. Aside from the construction side of the business, it has access to a further 5,000 previously owned properties. Royal Marbella Group in-house financial planning, mortgages, taxation services, legal advice and individually tailored inspection facilities enable its clients to make an informed decision. Royal Group's sports clients include Sir Geoff Hurst, Sir Steve Redgrave and Tony Underwood.

The Value Of An Icon

Introduction

Endorsements in sport are an essential part of the industry. They provide funding and income to athletes and elevate the profile of the brands involved. Often a brand will select an athlete based on current or expected success and will move on to other athletes when 'the next big thing' comes on the scene. Some brands can strike it lucky as Brylcreem did when they used a young David Beckham to help redefine the brand to a new and more youthful market. Sponsorship is not just about increasing sales, it is about creating a connection between the consumer and the brand. After consultation with leading sports agency, World Famous Group, I have come up with four sporting heroes' case outlines that will help define and emphasise the true value of an icon.

Sir Geoff Hurst

It is rare that someone becomes an icon. It is rarer still to be both an icon and a legend. Geoff Hurst had many achievements

in his illustrious football career including 24 goals for England in 49 appearances but is best known as the only footballer to score a hat-trick in a World Cup final. As part of the World Cup winning team, Geoff Hurst will always be linked to Kenneth Wolstenholme's commentary 'they think it's all over. It is now' as he sealed victory in 1966. In the autumn of 1998 the BBC announced that this goal has been the most shown and popular sporting piece of footage ever seen on television. Off the field Geoff has come to embody the spirit of that great squad that included Bobby Moore, Bobby Charlton

and Nobby Stiles. In a team full of soccer legends Geoff has become an icon for both his personal accomplishments and his pivotal role in an iconic moment in sporting history.

Eldrick 'Tiger' Woods

Although still in his 20s, Tiger Woods has already achieved iconic status since turning professional in 1996. The first person to hold the PGA championship, The Masters, the US Open Championship and British Open Championship titles simultaneously, Woods is arguably the greatest golfer of all time. Brands that associated themselves with him like Nike, American Express, TAG Heuer and Buick have benefited from the relationship. Consequently, the brands have built campaigns around his personality and success which has seen him transcend the golfing audience and become an international household name. His commitment to his sport and to his brand partners makes him a very desirable figure for marketeers. His close association with Nike has worked exceptionally well. He represents the core Nike brand attributes – 'active, inspired, intense, energized – a winner'.

Sir Steve Redgrave

His extraordinary achievement of a gold medal in five consecutive Olympic Games is a testament to the strength of character that has turned a great rower into a sporting icon. With a select number of endorsements including Flora, Royal Marbella Group and Walkers, Steve has focused on forming his own brand 5G. With reference to his five gold medals all his product ranges will satisfy his five gold principles; performance, durability, integrity, quality and value. Steve has managed to embody all the finest aspects of sportsmanship and his conduct on and off the water has made him an inspirational role model to many.

Ian Thorpe

Born in 1982, Ian already possesses the qualities that will see him remain a sporting icon long after he stops swimming. Australia's greatest ever athlete, he has won nine Olympic medals including five gold's, eleven world championship titles and has broken 22 world records. Prior to the 2002 Commonwealth games in Manchester Ian was chosen as an 'Icon of the Games' as he embodied the spirit of the competition. At the Games he went on to win six gold medals and one silver. Like most major athletes he is endorsed by a wide range of brands including Omega, adidas, Sony and Audi. Despite the obvious financial advantages that these sponsorships bring, the 'Thorpedo' remains unusually grounded. His focus has always been for the sport and it is this dedication that has elevated his public perception throughout the world.

Conclusion

It takes a very special individual to become an icon, especially in their lifetime. There has been much media hype about sports stars becoming stand alone brands. Athletes like Michael Jordan and David Beckham capitalise heavily on their name but while they are great athletes they would be very weak as brands with little strategy and a reliance on their performance. Some brands have been created like Fred Perry but mostly athletes and brands work better side by side via the endorsement route. The value of an association with an icon is hard to quantify as individual brands will have different objectives but it is safe to say that the benefits are not just short term financial goals. Benefits are also linked to the goodwill and personal value that is delivered by linking to an icon and showing a clear understanding and respect for his or her achievements.

SPORT ENGLAND

ROGER DRAPER

Chief Executive, Sport England
www.sportengland.org
Sport England is the organisation providing the strategic lead for the delivery of the Government's sporting agenda in this country, and is a distributor of lottery funds to sport. Its mission is: to work with others to create opportunities for people to get involved in sport, to stay in sport, and to excel and succeed in sport at every level. Sport England are the largest distributor of lottery and exchequer funding for sport in England, having invested over £2 billion since 1994. Its investment and work is guided by the strategic priorities of boosting participation in sport – particularly in disadvantaged areas – promoting equity in sport; and providing the infrastructure for developing world class sporting performers.

Evolving the Brand of Sport

Sport as a generic brand has many dimensions.

For the individual, sport can foster self-esteem, confidence and general well being. Sport helps us understand what it takes to be a winner and the value that comes from simply taking part – lessons that will stand us in good stead throughout our lives.

For some, sport has even more impact, it is an all-consuming passion that drives our top athletes to success on the world stage.

For society as a whole, sport and physical activity in the wider sense, can drive economic value, social cohesion, regeneration, crime reduction and, quite literally, the health of the nation – the issue of our time. With one in four adults and one in five children reportedly obese, pushing the health value of the sport brand has never been more important.

In recent years sport has had to evolve in response to changing demographics and trends in society. People are living and working longer. There are more single person households and in dual adult households, fewer of these adults are caring for children full time.

We are more time precious than ever before, and consequently more demanding of our leisure time. We also want instant gratification, excitement and escapism. And thanks to DVD and computer games we don't even need to get off the sofa to enjoy them – Play Sport is competing with Play Station.

Sport has had to recognise these trends and adapt what is on offer. These trends are both a threat to active participation, but also an opportunity if sport responds appropriately. In recent years we have seen the growth of 'extreme' sports, carefully nurturing their cool, leading edge brand values, catering for a new generation of individual thrill seekers.

Traditional sports have begun to cotton on, albeit slowly in some instances. Twenty20 cricket was a long time in the making, but what a phenomenal success it turned out to be in its first two seasons. A new generation of fans has been attracted by the shorter, more colourful and, dare we say it, more exciting version of this most traditional of sports. Let's hope this enthusiasm to watch translates into enthusiasm to play.

Another traditional sport has also caught the mood. Having already developed Mini Tennis for the 6-10 year olds, and Play Tennis to encourage the adult market to 'have a go' during the summer season, the Lawn Tennis Association (LTA) is all set to launch a new brand of the game targeted at the elusive teenage market. Raw Tennis taps into a need to have street credibility, a touch of glamour and will try to fit into the

already congested lifestyle of the aspiring adult. It is widely known that participation in sport drops sharply with the advent of adolescence. Getting this market to stay with it is a tough challenge and will only be overcome by astute product development that taps into the emotional psyche of the target audience. Raw Tennis is a laudable initiative and another step in the right direction for a governing body trying to broaden the appeal of its sport.

What is clear is that getting people active has to be at the heart of sports and therefore Sport England's agenda. This is reflected in our vision: making England an active and successful sporting nation. In our role as the Government's strategic lead for sport in England, we play a major part in creating the conditions in which the generic brand of sport can thrive and prosper. Earlier this year we published the Framework for Sport in England, setting out the strategic direction and policy priorities that sit behind our vision for sport.

Following on from this we have introduced a number of key strategic initiatives consistent with the vision and mindful of the social trends that have been described above. Our community sport

investment strategy now encourages a longer term and more rounded approach to facility development. The traditional notion of single sport clubs at single sport venues has to change. And indeed it is happening. There are already many great examples of the development of multi sport club environments where facilities are shared across a variety of user groups, and the users themselves are able to engage in a variety of activities. Multi sports clubs are the norm in much of the rest of continental Europe and evidence suggests they are key to sustainability – both of assets and of participation.

Sport is wising up to what people actually want – it is no use preaching that sport is a wonderful thing if all that is on offer is cold unfriendly leisure centres and muddy football pitches with shabby changing facilities. Sport as a brand has to reach out to many different types of people with very different interests.

Strategic planning is the key to future success. On a national basis we have kicked off a process that links funding to the production of robust Whole Sport Plans by the national governing bodies. The new process requires the administrators to plan the development of their sports at all levels, across a four-year business cycle. Crucially this must include how they will activate new participants as well as achieve success at the highest level. Each individual sport needs to think how it will build its own generic sport brand and how it will develop the brand to appeal to different market segments. Tennis, as described earlier, is showing the way.

Finally, we have also acknowledged that the marketing of sport and the benefits of physical activity should not be left to the sports alone. Social marketing campaigns in other fields, for example, highlighting the dangers of smoking, drugs, driving too fast and throwing fireworks, have all been successful in changing behaviours over time. Other countries, notably Canada, Germany and Australia, appear to have had success in changing attitudes to being active, through sustained campaigning over a number of years. During this summer we piloted an initiative in the North East of England called Everyday Sport, featuring a TV commercial, posters, local sporting and non sporting celebrities, and a range of on the ground activity designed to engage local organisations. The central idea was that a little more activity each day, in a way that suited the individual, was easily achievable and 'Every Body feels Better for it'.

The early results of this activity are encouraging and we will share the learnings with all the various stakeholders with a view to informing the development of a national campaign that would play a key part in helping us become a more active nation.

Our lifestyles are changing and the sports that change with the trends will be the ones that thrive and prosper through developing their brands to appeal to distinct target markets. Sport England will continue to encourage them to do this, whilst playing our own role in promoting the essential values of sport and increased physical activity, across all sectors of society.

RICHARD GILLIS

richard@gillisonline.co.uk
Richard Gillis is a freelance journalist writing about issues affecting the business of sport. He was formerly editor of SportBusiness International the market-leading publication for the professional sports industry.

Passion Play

The most interesting trend in relation to sports brands over the past five years has been the efforts made by governing bodies to build an identity of their own. Some have achieved it whilst others have just changed their logo.

Federations are the rule makers, the guardians of the game's history and responsible for nurturing its grass roots.

However, sport is about more than these things.

And the challenge of the governing bodies is to leverage value from the passion and the emotion that is such a part of sport's appeal. Unfortunately, it often seems that they are invisible when things go well and are a handy scapegoat during times of crisis, such as match-fixing allegations, drug scandals and tabloid sex cases.

At stake is the chance of a bit of open ground in the increasingly crowded sports market place, where events, teams and individual players jostle for the attentions of global sponsors, themselves keen to bask in sports reflected glory.

The governing bodies' trump card is that they own the means by which the stars become stars. It is this that has become their trading currency. The FA can reasonably argue that a fair chunk of Beckham's fame is built on his performances in an England shirt and that he is a world star because he appears in the World Cup, (now known as The FIFA World Cup).

The attribution of a person's image rights is a very tricky business, one which will keep the lawyers in work for some time, but it is obvious that by associating more closely with the big names the governing bodies can generate much needed income. It is this money that tends to those all-important grass roots.

Millions of pounds of sponsorship money flows toward the FA Cup, the Olympics and the Ryder Cup because they are great targeting tools which can deliver large audiences at a given time and place. Against the backdrop of media fragmentation, multi channel television and advertising avoidance devices such as Tivo, this is a promise other forms of marketing find difficult to match.

Because of this demand from sponsors, the price charged by federations such as FIFA, UEFA, NFL, Nascar and F1 has bucked the rest of the sport sponsorship market in maintaining its value. Another reason for the price tag is that these rights holders are each striving to increase the size of the global footprint of their events, opening up new territories to the sport and adding value to their commercial partners' investment.

UEFA estimates put the number of countries taking coverage of Euro 2004 at around 200, this figure is evidence of the emergence of the tournament as a genuinely global showcase. The American major leagues have also spent a great deal of time and money in their efforts to grow their own European strongholds, albeit to limited effect.

Updating a sport's brand requires administrators to move it along the line between sport and entertainment, opening it up to new audiences without undermining the core values that make it so compelling to the hardcore fans.

This is a challenge being faced by the English and Wales Cricket Board (ECB), and to which they have brought an innovative solution, Twenty20 Cricket.

And, it's a dirty great big hit. It has breathed life into the whole sport and helped it find some back page space, a rare thing indeed for domestic cricket in a tabloid newspaper market dominated by

football coverage. It will be interesting to monitor the impact of such a radical move on the brand of the ECB.

RICHARD (DICKIE) JEEPS CBE

Richard – affectionately known to many as Dickie – is a former England Rugby player and was Captain of England from 1960-62. Furthermore, he was the first English player to go on three British Lions tours (South Africa in 1955 and again in 1962 as well as Australia/New Zealand in 1959). Dickie has also played more Lions test matches than any other English player ever. Off the pitch, he was President of the RFU in 1976 and was also the Chairman of the UK Sports Council.

A Lifetime of Change in Rugby – Through the Eyes of a Legend

When I started playing rugby it was mainly a public school game with Oxford and Cambridge Universities having a big influence on international sides. We were amateurs – in fact we were given 50p a day in expenses when I was on the Lions tours in the 1950s.

My playing career started at Bedford Modern School, which

I left to join Cambridge City. Senior rugby in England was, at this point, run by the county system and I got in to the Eastern County side in 1950. Then, in 1954 I joined Northampton where I played for ten years. This was the normal route for international players at that time.

Looking back at rugby in the early 1950s the club houses and changing facilities were fairly primitive and not many clubs aspired to the wonderful club houses of today. Furthermore, there was no sponsorship at any level – even Twickenham had no advertising boards whatsoever.

The equipment of the day was also very different. The rugby balls we used to play with were made of leather. Even good quality balls were like sponges when they became full of water, so were difficult to handle and extremely heavy in wet conditions.

England, plus all the World Cup games now, are played with a Gilbert rugby ball. In my opinion, Gilbert have been the most standard ball. The modern ball does not absorb water and is easier to handle and much easier to kick consistently.

This in itself has changed the game, and now every team must have a Jonny Wilkinson!

Added to this, the laws of the game were very complicated when I was playing and they have been constantly evolving over the last 50 years. Nearly every year there is more 'tinkering' with the rules.

In the 1950s coaches were frowned upon – fitness training took place two nights a week on Tuesdays and Thursdays. Attendance was not compulsory and players could get a place on the side even if they didn't go. Today, there is a high standard of coaching as well as a good playing structure taking place on an international level. The referees are now also professionals, fitted with microphones linked to their touch judges and in some cases transmitted to the spectators. There is even an extra referee in the form of TV replays, used in the event of doubtful tries.

Unlike in my day, the modern international rugby player does not need a full time job. He must train very hard, keep incredibly high fitness levels and stay out of injury. He can wear body armour, or even gloves (not allowed and totally unheard of in my day).

1995 was an important year for Rugby. The international board declared overnight that rugby, against the odds, would go professional. Following this, all major players became contracted to the premier clubs. Sadly that did not include some of the much older clubs that had been established over 100 years previously and who had been the backbone of British rugby such as Richmond and Blackheath. These clubs are still around but fighting their way back up the league system.

England players up until 1995 all came from the county system but in 1995 when the premier division was started there was a complete turn around with the contracting of players to the premier division clubs. County rugby became a complete subsidiary. For the professional game to succeed, every club had to have major fund raising through sponsorship and if possible a major benefactor. The England team now comes from this premier division. Selection of the England side is now three deep. As a result the Premier Division lose a lot of their players to international teams training. Now in 2004 we are seeing a huge influx of overseas players – not only in the premiership but throughout rugby. This means that the premiership clubs do not

lose as many players to international sides, but also means that the opportunities for our grass routes younger players are much less.

When I played, gates at Northampton were around 5,000. Nowadays this is more like 13-14,000. Some clubs aspire to almost 20,000. I believe that the season is now much too busy. It used to be from September to April. Now the game is played after that period in addition to internationals being held.

In my day if you played for your country you could only get four caps a year and once every four years South Africa, Australia or New Zealand would arrive – allowing a possible 5th cap in that year. This season there are three pre-Christmas internationals, five international games after Christmas plus a Lions tour so today's

players can earn up to fifteen caps a year, even more in a World Cup year. The change in rules with regard to replacements also means that many more caps are available. Any player who sets foot on the pitch – even if only for two minutes – earns a cap!

England did brilliantly to win the World Cup and what it has done for the game has

made a huge growth in the numbers of youngsters wanting to play rugby.

What the game needs to do is to make sure that below the premiership there is a consistent way to feed the talented young players through the system to the very top – ensuring more of our home grown talent gets noticed. I also think that there has to be a balance between English and other players within the Premier division so that there is still room for the talented English players to climb the ladder of success.

Rugby has moved a hell of a long way since I first played for Cambridge City. Cambridge City itself is now a far more professional organisation with sponsorship, coaching, a great club house and a host of other modern facilities.

So, what does a school boy now need to do if he wants to play for his national side? Firstly, he needs to get fit, to join a club where he can demand a first team place and if he has real talent he can climb to a premiership club.

Crucially what I would like to see is a guarantee that English talent still has a priority place in English rugby.

NICK KELLER

Managing Director, Benchmark Sport & the Sport Industry Awards
www.benchmarksport.com

Benchmark Sport is a marketing, talent and event management agency that specialises in sport. Today it works alongside some of the biggest brands in the sports industry including the British Olympic Association, Rugby Football Union and Sport England. Its elite stable of athletes and sports personalities includes four Rugby World Cup Winners and two Olympic Gold Medallists. It is also owner and architect of the renowned Sport Industry Awards, now entering its fourth year and the cue for the industry to meet and reward commercial excellence in the business of sport.

Super 'Human' Brand

The jobs of brands and marketers today is the pursuit of Superbrand status. They do this by extracting what is positive about their product and seeking to forge a bond between it and the consumer. The consumer, for his or her part, is ready to form an emotional relationship if what's on offer is attractive. When this happens, the beer, the chocolate bar or the deodorant cease to be a product, they become friend, confidante and ally.

There is no market sector where this emotional brand chemistry can occur more potently than sport. Sport has always been a vehicle for its consumers' emotions – long before it became a business. It evokes devotion, loyalty, delirium, desperation, tears of happiness, tears of sadness. And even before the advent of the modern sporting superstar, most emotion was reserved for our heroes. They were the focal point of every consumer's emotional investment.

What is different today from the days of Matthews, Compton and Bannister is the commercial

environment. Modern media and marketing means today's sporting heroes – David Beckham, Wayne Rooney, Johnny Wilkinson, Michael Schumacher – are indisputably some of our most visible Sport BrandLeaders. Consumers invest in them the same way they invest in brands from other market sectors. Matthew Pinsett's tears, Jonny

Wilkinson's joy, Paula Radcliff's agony, Tim Henman's frustration, Kelly Holmes' disbelief are no longer the private property of these athletes. They are perceived by consumers to be theirs too.

Clearly from a commercial standpoint, there is great value to be extracted from the athlete's, or rather the brand's relationship with such an emotionally predisposed audience. And more and more companies recognise this golden opportunity. Here we are not just talking about sporting goods companies but global Sport BrandLeaders who invest in the Beckhams, the Woods and the Schumachers to fast track their product to hero status.

The consumer not only responds positively to the notion that the best use the best. But buying the product we are drawn closer to them. We feel that we know them better. By using the same product we become more like them and they become more like us.

You only have to look at the seminal piece of sports marketing in 2003 by adidas with Jonny and Becks to understand the real impact of the Sport BrandLeader on itself. The humanity and accessibility of the situation, essentially two lads having a kick-around in the local park, allowed us to reach out and touch our heroes. They were doing something that we've all done except, of course, they weren't. The genius was in allowing the consumer to believe that stars and mere mortals were for a short while one and the same.

Of course, the use of the Sport BrandLeaders – the sports personality – has to be handled with an element of caution. Not every professional sportsman has the talent or charisma to wear the mantle. Young men and women can be indiscreet, immature and volatile. Athletes have a limited shelf life before they must reinvent themselves as a commentator, a speaker, a presenter, a coach or a sponsor ambassador. As with any sponsorship, a company must choose the right person. But that is a detail rather than a principle.

What is clear is if your star athlete is recognisable, desirable, aspirational and capable of evoking strong emotion, then he or she can help you build a special and commercially rewarding relationship via sport with your consumer. When the latter believe that they were in part responsible for Jonny Wilkinson's drop goal, Europe winning the Ryder Cup and Becks' match-winning free-kick, you know they are ready to invest in the products that are associated with these Sport BrandLeaders.

STEVE MADINCEA

Founder & Group Managing Director, PRISM
www.prismteam.com

PRISM turns insight into action with its Brand Activation specialties. In Sponsorship Consultancy, PRISM's Brand Sponsorship Valuator 6.0 provides Six Sigma quantifiable results for blue chip brands' sponsorship investments. Actively engaged in Formula One, NASCAR, Champions League football and the Olympics since 1993, PRISM delivers Sports Marketing & PR impact for brands globally. PRISM also drives Product Launch momentum with award-winning work for global brands in telecoms, fuels, automotive and other sectors. And its Brand Experiences, including the PRISM-created Land Rover 'G4 Challenge' and Standard Chartered 'The Greatest Race on Earth', create ultimate connections with consumers for international brands.

The Future of Sport BrandLeaders

Sport BrandLeaders are taking a more prominent role in brand communications and life in general, and this trend shows signs of accelerating, based on recent data on consumer attitudes as well as the experiences of today's Sport BrandLeaders.

First let's look at some recent consumer trends. According to the sponsorship industry group IEG, expenditures in sponsorship have risen by an average of 6.4% from 2001 to 2004 despite the slow economy over this period in major markets such as the UK. The fact that sports expenditure has actually risen during this difficult period, while advertising and sales promotion have not increased as dramatically, tells us brands are turning more toward sports to connect with their key consumers.

Add to this the fact that last year consumers spent more money reaching out proactively to connect with brands (via the web, MP3 players etc) than brands spent trying to connect with consumers (via traditional advertising). One logical conclusion is that consumers are moving faster than brands and brand managers at trying to reach out and connect with Sport BrandLeaders.

Juan Carlos Perez, VP of Sponsorship at Shell Brands International, has observed these effects first-hand while working with a wide variety of Sport BrandLeaders. Perez sees the future quite clearly:

"The Shell brand is powerful by itself, but it does benefit from the associations we have developed through sports with Ferrari and Ducati. For the future, we need to expand those influential relationships to include markets and consumers which we may not have previously engaged. This can be done more quickly via Sport BrandLeaders than it can using traditional communication channels."

Pepsi has used sports sponsorship and Sport BrandLeaders like David Beckham as a cornerstone of their recent communication programmes. Pepsi's Beckham promotions are aggressive and innovative. Sport BrandLeaders of the future will be those who continue to develop the most creative connections with consumers, like the Pepsi Beckham World Cup promotion, which allowed consumers access to their heroes via the Pepsi brand. Sports brands will play an increasingly crucial role as an opportunity provider to consumers.

It's clear that Sport BrandLeaders can break down barriers faster than a multi-million-pound advertising campaign. Take Vodafone's sponsorship

League. But those that did, like Ford, have had their faith paid back many times over as the UEFA Champions League has grown as an outstanding consumer platform."

The future of Sport BrandLeaders is exciting and vibrant because the industry now has a track record of delivering results – something that it didn't have ten years ago. So given the above, what will future Sport BrandLeaders look like? Future Sport BrandLeaders are certain to have key traits, including being aggressive, innovative and willing to accept some risk to stay ahead of the competition. For brands willing to take this approach, sports can represent a considerable competitive advantage.

of the Ferrari Formula One team. Prior to the brand's involvement with Ferrari, Vodafone had sponsored activities like cricket that were viewed as UK-centric. Yet Vodafone wanted, and needed, to extend its brand association beyond the UK and portray itself as a more international company. By engaging with Ferrari via sponsorship, Vodafone would not only be involved with a leading Formula One team but it would also have a communication platform that easily transcended borders and language barriers. For Vodafone's international growth plans, it was a perfect fit.

Sport BrandLeaders need to be comfortable with a certain amount of risk. Take the UEFA Champions League, which is considered the most successful sports platform in Europe. In the inaugural 1992

season, not many companies were willing to take a leap of faith when the UEFA's Champions League marketing agency, T.E.A.M., came knocking on their door. Juergen Lenz, T.E.A.M.'s President, recalls those early days: "We approached every blue-chip brand in Europe. Most were unwilling to take the risk on the first year of the Champions

ALON SHULMAN

Chairman, World Famous Group
www.worldfamousgroup.com

WFG is a sports, music, film, events and entertainment marketing and management company. With headquarters in Chelsea Village, London, WFG operates internationally providing a diverse range of services to clients that includes individuals, institutions, brands and agencies. WFG also act as agents to a wide range of individuals and rights holders on an exclusive, non-exclusive or consultancy basis. World Famous Football operates as an agency for footballers and provide contract negotiation, commercial representation and personal management. WFF retains the exclusive services of a FIFA Licensed Players Agent.

Sponsorship and Brand Building in the Sports Sector

Introduction

The sports sector offers a brand high visibility and the opportunity to have an involvement with a large number of consumers. However, being a sports fan is about passion and not about business so any brand hoping to tap into this audience must first understand the emotive nature of sport and evaluate how to maximise the sponsorship experience for the brand, the sport and the fans.

Sponsorship helps build the loyalty of your consumers and thereby your profits by communicating with them more directly. Good sponsorship should promote better sales. The investment made not only has the possibility to increase sales but also the impression of added value it creates. Brand names and logos are now seen as company assets often with a value on the balance sheet. It is important to put these assets out to the market place.

There has been a dramatic rise in the reliance of promotion to encourage short-term sales – often at the expense of advertising and loyalty-building direct marketing. Paradoxically as sponsorship has increased so has the difficulty in maintaining the desired exposure. Despite sports sponsors effectively underwriting televised events, remote controls are used to surf away from adverts. This has meant that the presence of brands in televised sport has to be within the programme which involves more considered sponsorship and associated promotions.

On the Right Track

A well put together sponsorship strategy should benefit the brand away from the sporting arena. Further involvement is inevitable and comes with the territory of sponsorship. Promotions linking the sponsorship to the brand or product can reinforce the brand message. These promotions can range from in-store activity to advertising campaigns. Database-driven brand loyalty programmes can further enhance the strategic aspect of sponsorship. Databases can be used to vary the promotion from consumer to consumer thus providing the maximum return. In this way promotion can be

seen as an incentive for new customers and a 'thank you' for existing customers. Involving the consumer makes the brand identity stick and maintains the relationship away from the sport stronger. This is especially beneficial to brands whose message is not instant and who are selling a service as well as a product. Barclaycard's sponsorship of the FA Premier League (Barclaycard Premiership) has aided to position the brand as accessible, lively and friendly and helped prevent consumers being lured by new, young brands entering the market. From the outset, Barclaycard has recognised that to be a

successful sponsor a financial services brand has to earn the respect and acceptance of the fans both at the games and through the media. Barclaycard has made a £4 million commitment to the grass roots game which has created recognition that is unmatched by its peers.

Getting it Right

Coca-Cola is the world's most valuable and most recognised brand, worth an estimated US$72.5 billion in Interbrand's global brand league and has 94% global recognition. Sponsorship of major global events such as the Olympic Games and the FIFA World Cup ensures that the brand is present when nations come together on the international sporting stage. In football, Coca-Cola is a major sponsor of events like the FIFA World Cup and the UEFA European Championships as well as title sponsor of the UK football league for three seasons from the beginning of the 2004/05 season. The brand has remained true to its 'think local, act local' approach by supporting grassroots football throughout the UK and helping fans get

closer to the game. Like sponsorship, advertising must convince and motivate a potential consumer. Advertising campaigns like 'Eat football, Sleep Football, Drink Coca-Cola' have created a close link with the fans and the brand by sharing in the passion for the game on every level. Coca-Cola has always realised that consumer involvement is the key to greater loyalty and has encouraged participation on a national scale. Coca-Cola's sponsorship in sport, like its involvement in music, communicates the brand identity. Coca-Cola's sponsorship has created relationships with retailers and consumers as well as within the brand company itself.

Nearly Right is Totally Wrong

Often brand building is viewed as a cost rather than an investment. Even when sponsorship is done for the right reasons the brand must stack up. Sponsorship of a leading sport event is not sufficient to

make a brand good or successful. The sponsorship must also be right – when dealing with the emotive sports fan, nearly right is totally wrong.

Sponsorship cannot be evaluated on a conference room table, only in its natural sales environment. Good, well thought out and cleverly executed sponsorship gives the brand 'the advantage of difference' and a solid foundation from which to develop further and longer lasting relationships.

adidas
adidas UK Ltd
The adidas Centre
Pepper Road
Hazel Grove
Cheshire
SK7 5FD

Animal
Animal
Merchants House
Vanguard Road
Poole
Dorset
BH15 1PH

Athletics Weekly
Descartes Publishing
83 Park Road
Peterborough
PE1 2TN

Berghaus®
Berghaus Ltd
12 Colima Avenue
Sunderland Enterprise Park
Sunderland
Tyne & Wear
SR5 3XB

Bloc
Inline UK Ltd
The Base
Daux Road
Billingshurst
West Sussex
RH14 9SJ

Crewsaver
Crewsaver
Mumby Road
Gosport
Hampshire
PO12 1AQ

Eastpak
VF Northern Europe Ltd
Park Road East
Calverton
Nottingham
NG14 6GB

England Rugby
Rugby Football Union
Rugby House
Rugby Road
Twickenham
TW1 1DS

Eurosport
Eurosport Television Ltd
55 Drury Lane
London
WC2B 5SQ

FALKE
FALKE
Sports Division
P.O. Box 1109
57376 Schmallenberg
Germany

Fila
Fila UK (Authorised Distributor)
Proline International Ltd
Units 5 & 6
Colonial Business Park
Colonial Way
Watford
WD24 4PR

Grays
Grays of Cambridge International Ltd
Station Road
Robertsbridge
East Sussex
TN32 5DH

Harrows Darts
Harrows Darts
Cobra Unit 3
Pindar Road
Hoddesdon
Hertfordshire
EN11 0JX

Heineken Cup
ERC
Huguenot House
35-38 St Stephen's Green
Dublin 2
Ireland

howies
howies
Parc House
Parc Teifi Business Park
Cardigan
Dyfed
SA43 1EW

Kookaburra
Kookaburra Reader Ltd
3 Brakey Road
North Weldon Industrial Estate
Corby
Northamptonshire
NN17 1QY

Lord's
Marylebone Cricket Club
Lord's Ground
London
NW8 8QN

LTA
The Lawn Tennis Association
Palliser Road
West Kensington
London
W14 9EG

MCC
Marylebone Cricket Club
Lord's Ground
London
NW8 8QN

Millennium Stadium
Welsh Rugby Union Group
Golate House
101 Gt. Mary Street
Cardiff
CG10 1GE

Mitre
Mitre Sports International
Pentland House
Village Way
Wilmslow
Cheshire
SK9 2GH

Mizuno
Mizuno Corporation (UK)
Mizuno House
612 Reading Road
Winnersh
Wokingham
Berkshire
RG41 5HE

MotoGP
Dorna Sports, SL
Narcís Monturiol, 2
08960 Sant Just Desvern
(Barcelona)
Spain

Next Generation Clubs
Next Generation Clubs Ltd
Head Office
Mosquito Way
Hatfield Business Park
Hatfield
Hertfordshire
AL10 9AX

Nike
Nike UK
22 Gunton Street
London
W1F 2BY

PGA
The Professional Golfers'
Association
National Headquarters
Centenary House
The Belfry
Sutton Coldfield
West Midlands
B76 9PT

Prince
Prince Sports Europe Ltd
Thames House
116 High Street
Hampton Hill
Middlesex
TW12 1NT

Reebok
REEBOK UK
Moor Lane Mill
Lancaster
LA1 1GF

Russell Athletic
Mint Apparel Ltd
Unit 1
Colonial Business Park
Colonial Way
Watford
WD24 4PR

Science in Sport
SiS (Science in Sport) Ltd
Ashwood Laboratories
Brockhall Village
Blackburn
BB6 8BB

Scottish Rugby
Scottish Rugby
Murrayfield
Edinburgh
Scotland
EH12 5PJ

Shimano
Madison
Burnell House
8 Stanmore Hill
Stanmore
Middlesex
HA7 3BQ

Speedo
Speedo International
Ascot Road
Nottingham
NG8 5AJ

TaylorMade
TaylorMade – adidas Golf
TaylorMade Court
Jays Close
Viables Business Park
Basingstoke
RG22 4BS

Triumph
Triumph International Ltd
Arkwright Road
Groundwell
Swindon
Wiltshire
SN25 5BE

Twenty20 Cup
England & Wales Cricket Board
Lord's Cricket Ground
London
NW8 8QZ

Twickenham
Rugby Football Union
Rugby House
Rugby Road
Twickenham
TW1 1DS

UMBRO
UMBRO plc
Lakeside
Cheadle Royal
Cheshire
SK8 3GQ

Wilson
Sports Impact Ltd
Aston Court
31 Homefield Road
Wimbledon Village
London
SW19 4QF

Wimbledon
The All England Lawn Tennis Club
Church Road
Wimbledon
SW19 5AE